## Bar-B-Q Spareribs

meaty ribs - cut in serv
pieces. St oven at 4...
ch piece place thin sl...
... + slice of unpeel...
... Once r with
...pick. ...ac in shall...
...this pan - me 1 side...

## Sauce

1-1/2 cups sliced mushrooms
1 cup chopped
1/2 cup chopped
1/2 cup chopped onion
1 clove garlic, minced
3 T olive oil
1 1# 12-oz. can Italian
   plum tomatoes

1 8-oz can ...
... can ...
...rsley
...talian
salt & pepp...
1-1/2 cups
2 cups sli...

To make sauce, saute mushrooms, celery,
& garlic in oil for about 5 mins. Add
sauce, paste, seasonings, & one cup wa...
covered, for 1 hour. Add the zucchini
...lf cup water & simmer 15 mins longer
...ahead & refrigerate it overr...

## Zesty Green Rice

1 pt sour cream

2 T anchovie paste

4 sm. gr. scallions
   with tops 1/4

1 T vinegar

1/4 c. fresh chopped
   parsley

Cook rice wit
Chicken broth

**BITS**
**CREME**

...rves
...powder...
...onjuice
...n add
...slice
...until ... Bread

...sugar
...shortening
...gs
...vanilla
grated zucchini (unpeele...
flour
...sp. salt
...sp. soda

## Here's what's cookin:
## Eggplant Parmigiana
### Serves 6

Recipe from kitchen of J. Crescenzo

1 Medium EggPlant Peeled & sliced 1/4 to 1/2 "
1 Ball Motrazella Cheese
Tomato Sauce

Dip slices of Eggplant into:
   Egg & Milk mixture, then
   into seasoned breadcrumbs, then
   into flour. Repeat dipping
   into egg batter & bread...

...ry
on ...
onion...

Pour
1 3/4 ...
eggpl...

3 tsp cin...
...chopp...

## Recipe for Curry Dip

1 c. mayonaise
1 T. (scant) curry p...
2 T. horseradish...
1 T. terragon vin...
3/4 T. garlic salt
1 T. grated onio...
1 T. dry musta...

Combine ingredients
chill. For party, doubl...
recipe. Serve with ...
...Serve as a ...

# IN THE KITCHEN WITH BOB

## *My* Family's Best

# My Family's

# Best

## Bob Bowersox

*Food photographs by Mark Thomas Studio*

QVC PUBLISHING, INC.

QVC Publishing, Inc.
Jill Cohen, Vice President and Publisher
Ellen Bruzelius, General Manager
Sarah Butterworth, Editorial Director
Sue Dzieman, Executive Assistant

Produced in association with Patrick Filley Associates, Inc.
Design by Joel Avirom and Jason Snyder
Photography by Mark Thomas Studio
Prop styling by Nancy Micklin
Food styling by Rori Spinelli and Diane Vezza

**Q** Publishing and colophon are trademarks of QVC Publishing, Inc.

Published by QVC Publishing, Inc., 50 Main Street, Mt. Kisco, New York 10549

Manufactured in Hong Kong

ISBN: 1-928998-00-3

First Edition

10 9 8 7 6 5 4 3 2 1

# Contents

To all my families,
past, present and future.

# Acknowledgments

The first thank-you's go to QVC viewers, for your unwavering and enthusiastic support of my endeavors over the last twelve years. You are truly a family I feel a part of, and knowing you're always there gives me all the confidence I need to continue trying new things. I can't wait to see where we go next.

A very special thanks must go to Jill Cohen of QVC Publishing, an instant friend and confidante, and one of the savviest people I've ever met. You've proven to me many times that we speak the same language of quality, and I appreciate all you've done to help me with this, and other, projects. Thanks also to Ellen Bruzelius of the Publishing division—I've greatly appreciated your counsel.

Kudos to Patrick Filley of Patrick Filley Associates, a truly talented man, for the overall production management of this project. It looks spectacular, Patrick, and I've enjoyed the journey. By the way—when's my next deadline?

And thanks to the amazing team that makes *In the Kitchen with Bob* work week after week: Paula Bower, Melanie McCausland, Mary Dooner, Patti McGrath, Anthony Corrado, Harley Blaisdell, Kim, Carrie, Kevin, Mark, Steve, Michele, Amber and the countless Product Coordinators, Buyers, Directors, Line Producers and Control Room folks who help me make it look so easy. You're all magicians.

Thanks also to the senior management of QVC, Inc. for their continual support—Doug Briggs, Robb Cadigan, P.J. Baer-McGrath, Darlene Daggett, Rich Maurer, Barry O'Donnell and Jack Comstock—just a few among dozens.

And thanks every day to Toni and Taylor, the core and substance of what I now call my family. Without the two of you, none of this would have meaning.

Top Row, left: My maternal grandparents, Walter and Claire Fredericks (Papaw and Mamaw), Charleston, West Virginia; center: Papaw Fredericks, broadcasting on his radio station, WOBU, the first such station in West Virginia; right: My brother, Paul Bowersox; 2nd Row, left: Four generations of family: my daughter Taylor and her great-grandmother, Martha Marshall; center: My paternal grandfather, the Reverend Hixon Tracey Bowersox, pastor of St. Paul's Lutheran Church, Cumberland, Maryland; right: My first birthday—food was already an important part of life; 3rd Row, left: One of my favorite shots of Toni and me—relaxing at the beach; center: Mamaw Fredericks, in her matriarchal prime; right: My sister Maggie and her husband Ken; 4th Row, left: Some of the Wilson side of the family—Steve Wilson, Ron Duhon and Sue Wilson (the Cajun connection); right: Two of my most loved and respected women—my wife Toni and my mom Marilee

7

# Introduction

You know, it's funny sometimes. You go about a task—defining it, planning it, pulling its many elements together, looking at it from every conceivable point of view, designing it, writing it, discussing it...you think you know what you have, why you're doing it, what its purpose is. And then, in a split second, a sudden, breathtaking moment of clarity, you realize that what you have isn't at all what you thought you had. You see it for what it really is.

So it was with the compiling and writing of this book. *My Family's Best* was planned to be the follow-up to my successful first book, *In the Kitchen with Bob.* That first book presented recipes created for my television show of the same name which airs every Sunday on QVC. The included recipes were more gourmet fare, quick and easy versions of dishes I would have served in my restaurant. For this second book, however, I thought I'd get a little more personal with you, and bring together some recipes that I grew up with—dishes that you've heard me speak of on-air created by people I've mentioned fondly in passing. A collection of family-style recipes, basically.

Then came the breathtaking moment of clarity. As I sat at my desk looking over the completed manuscript, I suddenly realized that what I held in my hands was not simply a "collection of family-style recipes." It was so much more than that. What I had in my hands—and that you now hold in yours—was nothing less than my culinary inheritance. A legacy of smells and flavors, textures and colors, and even more than those, the memories—visual and aural—of the people who created them or preserved them through the years. But in addition to that, and maybe even more importantly, this book will become my legacy to my daughter Taylor. For now these recipes will never be misplaced or lost. Nor will the stories and memories of the people connected with them—the great-grandparents, grandparents, mothers, fathers, sisters, brothers, in-laws. The richness of a family's love affair with food will be passed on.

You see, food has always been a big thing in my family. Everybody cooked. Or baked. Or roasted. Or sautéed. Everyone developed a specialty of sorts. My grandmother made the best pies, cobblers and buckles in the world. My mother had no equal when it came to chicken or turkey.

My dad was the best baker I ever met. Even my great-grandfather, Frank Bowersox, an honest-to-gosh, hammer-swinging blacksmith in Cumberland, Maryland, did some terrific things with chestnuts (believe it or not).

And the current generation is no slouch either. My wife Toni and her grandmother Martha have brought the rich Italian and Polish traditions of their families to our table (Martha's one of those gifted cooks who measures everything by hand and gets it right every time). My Aunt Jeanne brings in the Scot, my cousins Linda and Sue the rich heritage of the Estonian and the Cajun, and my brother-in-law Ken a world palate, particularly the Asian. We are a vibrant, growing family that remembers and holds the cuisine of those who came before us as vital as their memories. Which is why it is important to us that we continue to master and pass along the rich legacy of family recipes left us.

Food, and the enjoyment of it, is a primary endeavor for my family, almost a ritual of sorts. Dinner, for instance, was (and still is with my own family today) a command performance. You were expected home every night at five-thirty for dinner, even if you arrived at five-twenty-five and left again at six. My mother would accept no excuses, whines or whimpers. You were there, period. It was the time the family gathered together as a unit, discussed the day's experiences, and planned tomorrow's. Not that any of us ever argued about having to be there, even as teenagers. Quite the contrary. We always wanted to be around that table because of what was on it.

My mother's cooking—traditional, but with a southern touch—was rich in texture, warm with flavor, wrapped in that indescribable..."something"...that a great cooking mother is able to impart to her food. She

Top: Toni and me on our tenth wedding anniversary

Bottom: Marilee and Don Bowersox
(Mom and Dad) about a year before I was born

9

Marilee and Don Bowersox
(Mom and Dad) about the time
my daughter Taylor was born

inherited a lot of her talents from her mother, my "Mamaw," who was a master of the American family cuisine, able to quickly turn whatever my grandfather brought in fresh from his nursery garden into meals no gourmet chef, regardless of his or her training, will ever be able to equal—profoundly rich, three-dimensional dishes, the thought of which instantly makes me salivate. These two women were masters of it all—from sinful dips to barbecued ribs to garlic-roasted lamb to soufflés and pies and cakes, and a chocolate fudge so rich it sticks your tongue to the roof of your mouth. I've included most of their masterpieces here.

And talk about ritual. Baking for my father was nothing short of religious. I will never lose the image of him retiring to the kitchen several nights a month, his hair askew, his glasses perched on the tip of his nose, with his robes (his full-length, wrap-around chef's apron), his sacrament (a small glass of vodka on the rocks with a twist), and his choir (the local classical music station, softly filling the room with Mozart, Bach or Beethoven). And the things that came out of that kitchen! Soups that were so thick and deep with taste and texture, a local shelter asked him to make them for their needy. Breads of all types that were so good, we all sat around the kitchen table waiting for them to come out of the oven so we could devour them before they cooled. Pasta sauces that would make an Italian grandmother weep (they actually did on one occasion).

Dad was also the keeper of the family legacy of desserts, some of which go back generations. He created a treasure box of such recipes, filled with gems from my grandmothers and great-aunts on both sides, women who

My brother Paul in
(where else?) the kitchen

understood the mysterious secrets of pies, cakes, cobblers, cookies and puddings. And the true value of those cards is that they not only contained the ingredients, but the techniques these remarkable women were taught by their mothers and their mothers before them.

I have built some of these secrets into the recipes included here. With Dad's passing, my brother Paul donned the mantle of "Dessert Master" in our family, building on the foundation my father and his relatives laid for him. By including several of Paul's seductive creations, I connect the past with the present.

And it's that connection to the past that jumped out at me when I looked through this finished manuscript. These recipes have become larger than the familial ritual and love of food that have sustained them through the generations. They are my way of touching those members of our family so long gone now. I make the Blueberry Buckle, and I can smell Mamaw's kitchen in West Virginia. I make the Italian Wedding Soup and I can hear the animated chatter in Toni's aunt's house in the Little Italy section of her hometown. I make the Sourdough Cheese Bread, and I can see my dad kneading the dough in the corner of his kitchen, hair tousled, glasses on the tip of his nose, and I hear Beethoven.

And this book, having been pieced together from my many inheritances, now becomes the legacy for my families. For my daughter Taylor, it will connect our past through my present into her future. And thanks to QVC, you—my extended family—can participate in this legacy of good food as well. You've heard me talk about these people and their recipes on-air for years, almost as if we'd been sharing family stories over a cup of coffee in your kitchen. You know me, and my family, almost as if we were your own family.

So, consider this book my way of handing you the Bowersox recipe box and saying, "Take what you want. There's not a bad one in the bunch." And by all means, pass them on. They are, after all, an inheritance.

The only surviving photo of my restaurant, The Crepe Chalet, in 1979

# STARTERS

Baked Zucchini-Garlic Squares

Spiced Nuts

Jezebel

Hot Crab Dip

Iris's Avocado Dip

Paul's Salsa

Jan's Crostini

Curry Dip

Tomatoes, Mozzarella
and Peppers

Crab Roll-Ups

Toni's Chicken Soup

Bowersox Onion Soup

Italian Wedding Soup

Dad's Vichyssoise

Quick Cold Beet Soup

Patricia's World Famous
Ginger-Carrot Bisque

# Baked Zucchini-Garlic Squares

*ANYONE WHO KNOWS my family knows we have garlic for blood. We'll put it in everything just to see what happens, and usually with good results. This was originally a recipe for zucchini squares, a run-of-the-mill recipe that Mom picked up at church. Dad couldn't leave well enough alone, of course, but no one's complained about his dabbling in 30 years. I don't think you will either.*

1 cup Bisquick

3 cups thinly sliced zucchini rounds

½ cup finely chopped onion (white or yellow)

4 garlic cloves, minced

4 eggs, beaten

½ cup vegetable oil

2 tablespoons chopped fresh parsley

½ teaspoon salt
   Dash of freshly ground pepper

½ teaspoon Lawry's Seasoned Salt (optional)

½ teaspoon marjoram

½ cup grated Parmesan cheese

Place the Bisquick, zucchini rounds, onion and garlic in a large bowl. Beat the oil into the eggs, then add to the bowl and toss the vegetables to coat. Add the parsley, salt, pepper, seasoned salt (if using), marjoram and Parmesan cheese. Toss again to coat.

Pour the contents of the bowl into a greased 13 x 9-inch baking pan, making sure that the zucchini is evenly spread through the pan. Bake for 30 minutes in a preheated 350°F oven.

Remove from the oven and cool for about 15 minutes on a rack. When sufficiently cooled, cut into 1- to 2-inch squares. Stack in a pyramid when serving.

# Spiced Nuts

*I SPENT MY LATE TEEN YEARS in Sharpley, a suburban neighborhood in Wilmington, Delaware. It was a tight-knit place, where all the dads worked for chemical giant DuPont, and all the moms were homemakers and stellar cooks. It was also a hotbed of recipe swappers. I think half the delicacies in the family recipe box were added during those years. This little curiosity, a crunchy explosion of sweetness and spice for holiday tables and picnics, came from the Gotsch family down the street, whose dad was my father's best friend at the time.*

¾ cup sugar

¾ teaspoon salt

1 teaspoon ground cinnamon

½ teaspoon ground cloves

¼ teaspoon allspice

¼ teaspoon ground nutmeg or freshly grated

1 egg white, slightly beaten

2½ tablespoons water

3 to 4 cups nuts (almonds, cashews, peanuts or a mix of them all)

Mix the sugar and the spices. Gently add in the egg white and the water, blending thoroughly with a whisk or fork.

Add the nuts, a half cup at a time. Stir with a fork until well coated. Lift out with forks and place on a lightly greased or nonstick cookie sheet. Bake in a preheated 275°F oven for about 45 minutes. Remove from oven and cool for 15 minutes. Store in a covered container.

# Jezebel

MAKES ABOUT 5 CUPS

*JUST MENTION JEZEBEL to my sister Maggie, and she moans with pleasure. No kidding—I tried it the other day. She uses it on just about anything, too—her morning toast, her afternoon sandwich, her dinner chicken entrée. It makes a terrific finger food for a buffet table (its original use), especially if you want to put out something that no one else has tried before. Now, I don't know if you'll be as devoted to Jezebel as Maggie is, but I bet you moan with pleasure a little.*

1  18-ounce jar apple jelly

1  18-ounce jar pineapple preserves

5  ounces horseradish (creamed or sauce)

1  teaspoon freshly ground pepper

3  teaspoons dry mustard

1  8-ounce package cream cheese

Wheat Thin crackers

Mix the first 5 ingredients and let stand for 1 hour. Can be stored in refrigerator until needed.

Place the cream cheese in the center of a serving dish. Pour the Jezebel sauce over the top. Serve with the crackers.

NOTE: Jezebel can also be used as a spread on toast or for sandwiches, or as a fabulous glaze for chicken or steak.

*Maggie, age 4, and me, age 5, growing up in West Virginia*

# Hot Crab Dip

MAKES 25 2-OUNCE DOLLOPS ON TOAST ROUNDS

*ONE OF THE INTERESTING SIDENOTES to the treasure box of recipes I inherited from my parents is the number of different handwritings the recipes are in. I can recognize most of those hands that are immediate family, but there are some that I have no idea about. This recipe (top, page 19) is one of those—a treasure in the box left by someone who'd crossed my parents' threshhold as mute proof that they'd been there. This dip is so good that I'd love to find its author and thank them, but since I'm unable to do that, I'll just honor their gift by passing it along to you. The Hot Crab Dip can be made stovetop and then placed in a chafing dish for a buffet.*

3  8-ounce packages cream cheese

½  cup mayonnaise

2  teaspoons prepared mustard
   (Dijon is O.K.)

1  teaspoon onion juice

1  teaspoon Lawry's Seasoned Salt

2  teaspoons confectioner's sugar

½  cup white wine

3  6-ounce cans or packages crabmeat,
   drained, picked over

1  loaf French bread, cut into
   ¼-inch-thick rounds

Melt the cream cheese in a double boiler over medium heat. Blend in the mayonnaise, seasonings, sugar and the wine.

Carefully flake the crab and then fold into the sauce in the double boiler. Heat until warm, and then serve with small, thin, toasted rounds of French bread. Can be placed in a heated bowl or in a chafing dish to be kept warm.

# Iris's Avocado Dip

*IRIS IS MY WIFE TONI'S AUNT, though they aren't that far apart in age. She loves great food and wine and plays a mean game of Scrabble. This (bottom, page 19) is one of the gifts she gave Toni years ago...a dip so easy to make and yet so addictively delicious that it's become a staple at any gathering of friends we have.*

2 medium or 1 large ripe avocado, peeled, mashed

½ small onion, finely chopped

1 large garlic clove, finely minced

½ firm tomato, finely chopped

Juice of 1 lime

Salt and freshly ground pepper to taste

Peel the avocado and slice the fruit into a medium bowl. Mash it with a spoon until it is soft and smooth. Add the onion, garlic and tomatoes and stir. Add the remaining ingredients to taste and stir well. Serve with nacho chips.

Toni's aunt, Iris, though she's actually more like a sister

# Paul's Salsa

MAKES 4 TO 5 CUPS

*I WAS FIRST INTRODUCED to my brother's salsa in the summer of 1997. We'd arranged a family reunion for about 30 of the extended family, and every family unit was commissioned to bring a different dish. Paul brought this salsa. He served it with tortilla chips and thin bread rounds (which almost made it seem like crostini). It was the hit of the reunion. Problem was, it was gone before we knew it. I guess we'll have to plan another reunion.*

8  tomatoes, finely chopped

2  large green chili peppers, finely chopped

2  medium or 1 large red onion, finely chopped

1  medium bunch cilantro, finely chopped

3  seranno or jalapeño peppers, finely chopped

Juice of 6 limes

1  tablespoon salt or to taste

Place all ingredients except the lime juice and salt in a bowl and stir to blend. Add the lime juice and the salt last. This salsa is best served immediately.

NOTE: You can use a food processor to make this quickly if you prefer. Just place all ingredients in the processor and chop until well mixed.

My brother, Paul,
and my aunt, Jeanne

# Jan's Crostini

*JAN MULLER IS A FAMILIAR FACE to QVC viewers. He's the spokesperson for a wide range of products, from Duralon and Circulon cookware, to the V-Slicer and Teba appliances. I met Jan professionally through QVC, of course, but we've become very good personal friends since, spending many a wonderful evening at each other's homes, cooking and savoring foods and friendships. Jan is a startlingly good cook, and an adventurous one as well. At one dinner together, Jan was responsible for the appetizer, and these crostini are what he came up with. They're fabulous, and became an instant favorite with our family. You can't go wrong starting out with these.*

2   tablespoons extra-virgin olive oil

1   large red onion, sliced into thin rings

1   3-ounce jar capers

    Truffle oil* or good extra-virgin olive oil

1   medium block dry ricotta cheese

4   to 6 figs, sliced

1   loaf hard-crusted Italian bread, sliced into ¼- to ⅜-inch-thick rounds

\*   *Truffle oil is available in specialty food shops.*

In 2 separate sauté pans or medium skillets over medium-high heat, warm about 1 tablespoon of olive oil. In 1 pan, sauté the red onion rings until soft and fragrant. In the other, sauté the capers until just slightly browned.

Meanwhile, toast the bread rounds just before building the crostini.

Build each crostini as follows: Brush the warm round of bread with a little truffle oil. Spread a layer of the dry ricotta cheese on top of the oiled breads. Top that with a fig slice or 2, then a tablespoon or so of the sautéed red onions, then a teaspoon or so of the capers. Consume immediately.

# Curry Dip

MAKES 1 ⅓ CUPS

*CONTRARY TO POPULAR BELIEF, "curry" is not an Indian dish, but a British one. To be sure, Indian cuisine has a similar dish, but the British popularized the spicy dish in the mid-1800s. Though this has a little bite, it's not a scorcher, and I think you'll find it an interesting addition to a party table. It was one of my parents' favorites.*

1 cup mayonnaise

1 tablespoon curry powder

2 tablespoons horseradish

1 tablespoon tarragon vinegar

¾ tablespoon garlic salt

1 tablespoon grated onion

1 tablespoon dry mustard

Combine all the ingredients in a bowl and blend thoroughly. Pour into a serving bowl, then chill before using. Serve with raw vegetables or as a sauce with meats or chicken.

My folks, Marilee and Don

# Tomatoes, Mozzarella and Peppers

MAKES 4 SERVINGS

*THERE IS ONLY ONE APPETIZER you'll see on my brother Paul's table when he's serving you pasta for dinner. He calls it his "Super Simple Italian Appetizer," but I thought we should be more descriptive. The "super simple" comes in on the preparation side. It takes only a couple of minutes to make. But the taste! It's fresh and light, yet at the same time complex. If you like mozzarella, you've just found your dish.*

2 large meaty tomatoes
Salt and freshly ground pepper to taste

1 round good all-milk mozzarella cheese, room temperature

1 12-ounce jar roasted red peppers

10 basil leaves, chopped
Olive oil (one flavored with garlic is best)

Slice the tomatoes ½-inch thick and lay out on a serving dish. Sprinkle the tomatoes with a little salt and pepper to taste. Slice the mozzarella into ¼-inch-thick rounds and layer on top of the tomatoes.

Spread some of the red peppers on top of the cheese, then sprinkle with a little of the chopped basil. Drizzle olive oil over all. Serve cool.

# Crab Roll-Ups

*THIS IS A REALLY OLD RECIPE, probably hailing back to my grandfather's days in Maryland. But I never had it as a child, because after my birth, my mother was never able to eat shellfish again (some kind of allergic reaction brought on by the pregnancy). It's a great buffet food, though, easy to make, and easy for people to pick up and eat. If you love crab, you'll love these.*

1 package refrigerated crescent rolls

1 pound fresh lump crabmeat, drained, picked over

¾ cup grated cheese (Cheddar, Monterey Jack or Parmesan)

2 tablespoons minced onion

Salt and freshly ground pepper to taste

Separate the individual sections of the crescent rolls and lay out on the work surface. In a glass bowl, lightly mix the crab and grated cheese.

Sprinkle each section with a little onion, salt and pepper. Using a teaspoon, place equal amounts of the crab and cheese mixture on each of the sections, spread evenly over its area. Roll each section up, starting from the wide end.

Place the roll-ups on a nonstick baking sheet, point side down and bake in a preheated 375°F oven for about 12 to 15 minutes, or until browned. Serve warm.

# Toni's Chicken Soup

*YOU KNOW HOW YOU HAVE childhood memories of dishes your mom made that you think are the best that have ever been made? That no other recipe will ever come close to? That when you think of your mom's cooking, you think of that one recipe? Well, I think this is the one recipe of her mom's that my daughter Taylor will remember all her life. There isn't a week that goes by without Toni making this soup for us, and there isn't a better one as far as we're concerned.*

1  4- to 6-pound chicken
   Water to cover chicken in pot
3  large carrots, cut into 2-inch pieces
2  celery ribs, cut into 2-inch pieces
2  to 3 onions, quartered (with root intact but trimmed)
1  teaball whole black peppercorns
1  10- to 12-ounce package fine egg noodles, cooked, drained

Clean the chicken well. If you want to cut down on the fat content of the soup, remove all the skin except for that on the wings and the back. This will, however, remove some of the chicken flavor from the soup. Place the chicken in a large stockpot and surround with the carrot, celery and the onions. Toss in the teaball of black peppercorns and add enough water to cover all. Cook for at least 1 hour on enough heat to force pot to simmer well.

When the soup is ready to serve, boil and drain the egg noodles according to the package directions. Place a layer of noodles in the bottom of each bowl.

Remove the chicken from the pot and place on a cutting board or platter. Cut several pieces of chicken (white or dark, depending on what your diners desire) and place them on the noodles. Ladle broth and vegetables on top of that to fill the bowl. Serve immediately.

# Bowersox Onion Soup

*ONE OF THE GREAT TASTES that came out of the Bowersox kitchens of my youth was my dad's onion soup. He worked for years to perfect it, and anyone who's tried it agrees that he achieved his goal. Of all the soups I included in my first cookbook,* In the Kitchen with Bob, *I have received more comments on Dad's onion soup than any other. However, in the intervening years, my wife and I have given up eating red meats, and that forced me to experiment with the soup to find a suitable replacement for the beef consommé. Give this one a try. I don't think you'll notice the changes, as that rich onion flavor that Dad perfected still comes through unadulterated.*

8   medium to large red onions

4   tablespoons unsalted butter

2   10¾-ounce cans concentrated chicken broth

1½  10¾-ounce cans water

½   teaspoon salt

1   teaspoon Worcestershire sauce

½   loaf French bread, cut into 2-inch-thick rounds

Mozzarella or Provolone (Dad's choice) cheese, thinly sliced

Freshly grated Parmesan cheese

Cut the onions into ⅜-inch slices, then cut the slices in half.

In a 4-quart stockpot or Dutch oven, sauté the onions in the butter. Do this very slowly, over a medium heat until deep, dark brown, with a thickened, almost caramelized texture without being burned. This can take anywhere from 20 to 40 minutes.

Add the chicken broth, water, salt and Worcestershire sauce and simmer until hot. Preheat the broiler.

Place 1 piece of the French bread in individual ramekins or high-sided, broiler-safe bowls. Ladle the soup over the bread until it is covered and the soup is near the top of the ramekins or bowls. Cover the ramekins or bowls with the cheese (2 to 3 slices for each ramekin), and place under the broiler until the cheese is melted and beginning to brown on top. Serve with the grated cheese to sprinkle over the top.

# Italian Wedding Soup

MAKES 12 10-OUNCE SERVINGS

*THIS IS A COMPILATION of recipes that come from the several Italian families on my wife's side. I suppose I could have called it "Sadie's Wedding Soup," after Toni's Aunt Sadie Cofrancesco, who supplied the bulk of the recipe, but then Aunts Edith, Vera, Mary, Geri, Dottie and Myrtle would have taken offence, saying it wasn't true to their recipe. You see, every Italian family has a recipe for this soup. And while they're all great, they're all different. So let's just keep the peace, call it by its generic name and extend our thanks to all of Toni's aunts.*

**BREAD**

- 8 eggs
- 3 tablespoons minced fresh parsley
- 1 cup grated Parmesan cheese
- 4 tablespoons flour
- 2 teaspoons baking powder
- Freshly ground pepper to taste

**MEATBALLS**

- 1 pound ground sirloin or ground turkey
- ½ cup breadcrumbs
- 1 teaspoon garlic powder
- 1 tablespoon finely chopped onion
- ½ teaspoon salt or to taste
- ¼ teaspoon freshly ground pepper

**BROTH**

- 2½ to 3 quarts chicken broth (homemade or 2 46-ounce cans)
- 2 10-ounce packages chopped spinach

**FOR BREAD:** Beat all the ingredients together in a mixing bowl, then pour into a greased and lightly floured cookie sheet with sides high enough to contain the liquid. Bake in a preheated 350°F oven for 5 to 10 minutes. Remove and cool on a rack, then cut into ½-inch squares and set aside.

**FOR MEATBALLS:** Mix all the ingredients together by hand in a large mixing bowl. Roll into small, dime-size meatballs. Place on a cookie sheet and bake for 5 minutes in a preheated 350°F oven.

**FOR BROTH:** Bring broth to a boil over medium-high heat and add the spinach. Then drop the heat to medium, and add the meatballs. Heat the soup to serving temperature. Place the bread cubes in a serving bowl on the table, along with a bowl of grated Parmesan or Romano cheese. Serve the soup in bowls—the diners will add the bread and cheese they desire.

# Dad's Vichyssoise

MAKES 5 CUPS

*MY DAD, DON BOWERSOX, loved a good soup. After he retired from DuPont, he spent his remaining years in the kitchen, learning the art of soup making and break baking (I've included some of his bread masterpieces later in this book). He developed some of the finest soups in my personal repertoire today, including this vichyssoise. I love cold soups, and am always trying to come up with new ones or improve old ones. But I haven't found one thing to improve upon in this recipe, which says a lot for the perfection of its creation.*

1   cup chopped leeks (white parts only)

⅓   cup diced green onions (white parts only)

4   to 5 tablespoons unsalted butter

2   cups peeled, finely diced potatoes

4   cups chicken stock

1   cucumber, peeled, diced

1   teaspoon dry mustard

1   teaspoon salt or to taste

1   teaspoon white pepper or to taste

1   to 2 cups cream

Chopped watercress or chives for garnish

Soak the leeks to remove the dirt. In a large stockpot or Dutch oven, sauté the leeks and green onions in the butter until softened, about 3 minutes. Add the potatoes and the chicken stock, bring to a boil, then drop the heat and simmer for about 20 minutes, or until the potatoes are softened.

Add the cucumber and cook at a simmer for 5 minutes more. Remove from the heat and let cool for about 10 minutes.

Skim any fat from the soup, then pour into a blender or food processor and puree. Strain through a metal strainer, then strain through cheesecloth. If grainy, put through the cloth again. Pour into a large bowl, add the spices and the cream, then chill thoroughly before serving. Garnish with chopped watercress or chives before serving.

# Quick Cold Beet Soup

MAKES 4 CUPS

*THIS SOUP COMES FROM MY SISTER Maggie, who lives in Denver, Colorado. Like the rest of the family, Maggie loves a good soup, and like me, she loves a good cold soup. But good, easy recipes for cold soups are hard to find. As fate would have it, my wife Toni is half Polish, and grew up with beet soups. She has given this one her blessing (even though it comes from a German girl in Denver). It's a great soup for a hot, humid summer day, and a terrific way to put a light beginning on a heavy dinner.*

2  15-ounce jars cooked peeled beets

1  to 2 small cucumbers, peeled, diced

2  to 3 green onions (white and green parts), diced

½  teaspoon dried dill

1  garlic clove, finely minced

Dash red wine vinegar

Salt and freshly ground pepper to taste

Sour cream for garnish

Put the beets, cucumbers and green onions in a food processor or blender and liquify into a rich, thickened liquid. Pour into a serving bowl.

Add the dill, garlic, vinegar and salt and pepper to taste. Stir well to blend.

Chill well, and serve cold with a dollop of sour cream in the center of each individual serving bowl.

# Patricia's World Famous Ginger-Carrot Bisque

MAKES 10 8-OUNCE SERVINGS

*THIS IS A RECIPE GENEROUSLY SHARED with me by QVC show host Patricia Bastia, and it has become a favorite. Patricia tells me that the soup is a Thanksgiving tradition in her family. It has fast become one for mine as well.*

¼ cup unsalted butter

2 pounds carrots, peeled, thinly sliced

2 large onions, finely chopped

5 cups chicken broth

1 tablespoon grated fresh ginger

½ teaspoon ground coriander

2 teaspoons grated orange peel

1½ teaspoons salt

Freshly ground pepper to taste

1 cup half-and-half or, for a creamier bisque, heavy cream

Sauté the carrots and onions in the butter until they soften. Add half the chicken broth and bring to a simmer for about 6 to 8 minutes.

Working in batches, puree the soup in a blender or food processor, and return to a stockpot. Add the remaining chicken broth, the spices, orange peel, salt and pepper. Add the half-and-half or cream, and warm (do not boil after the cream has been added—bring only to serving temperature).

# MAIN COURSES

Granny's Pot Roast

German Wrapped
    Hamburgers

Hot Chicken Salad

Beef and Vegetable Kebabs

Oven-Broiled
    Barbecue Chicken

Mom's Homemade
    BBQ Spareribs

Southwest Chicken Rolls

Iris's Vegetarian Pizza

Gilbert Hall Chili

Toni's Peppers and Pasta

Coquilles St. Jacques Crepes

Veal Marengo

Linguini with Sun-Dried
    Tomato Sauce

Tuna Soufflé

Jalapeño Chicken

Don's Homemade
    Pasta Sauce

Salmon Rolls with
    Horseradish-Dill Stuffing

Chinese Cashew
    Chicken Casserole

Garden Lasagne

Individual Shrimp and
    Zucchini Casseroles

Nut-Crusted Chicken Breasts
    with Mustard Sauce

Don's Pesto Spaghetti

Shrimp and Potato Gumbo

Mrs. C's Eggplant
    Parmagiano

Sautéed Scallops with
    Garlic-Balsamic Glaze

Granny's Crab Cakes

# Granny's Pot Roast

MAKES 6 SERVINGS

*TONI'S GRANDMOTHER, Martha Marshall, is an 80-something Polish grandmother who has more remarkably good recipes in her head than I have in my entire collection of books. Whenever we're planning to visit her, she always knows what we want for dinner. Toni loves her grandmother's pot roast, and I have to admit, I've never tasted better. It has something to do with the way the meat dissolves on your tongue, and the way the flavors of the meat and vegetables blend in an indescribable way. Though I've sworn off red meat for the last two years, I allow myself to fall off the wagon for Granny's Pot Roast.*

4 pounds boneless chuck, trimmed of excess fat

2 to 3 tablespoons vegetable oil

1 celery rib, chopped

1 medium onion, chopped

4 to 5 cups water

4 carrots, cut into 2-inch lengths

4 large potatoes, chunked

1 cube beef bouillon

1 cube chicken bouillon

1 tablespoon flour for gravy

In a large, high-sided skillet over medium-high heat, warm the oil, then add the roast and brown on both sides. Remove and set aside momentarily.

Add the celery and onion to the pan drippings and sauté them until the onion is wilted. Add the meat back to the pan and add the water. Cover the skillet and cook over medium-low to medium heat (whatever gives you a simmer on your stove) for 2 hours.

After the meat has simmered for the 2 hours, add the carrots and potatoes to the pan, nestling them into the gravy around the meat, and cook for another hour, or until the vegetables are fork-tender.

Remove the meat and vegetables to a serving platter and keep warm, then make the gravy. Add both bouillon cubes and stir to dissolve. Then put 1 tablespoon of flour into ¼ cup cold water. Whisk until dissolved, then add to the gravy and stir well to incorporate. Repeat the flour/liquid process as many times as needed to attain a gravy of desired thickness and consistency. Serve immediately.

# German Wrapped Hamburgers

*My ORIGINAL FAMILY NAME was Bauer-Saches, which is German for "farmer from Saxony." With an ancestry as Teutonic as that, you would figure there'd be a few Germanic trifles in the family recipe tin. Here's one for you that we kids used to love to help make as well as eat. I suppose it's the German twist on the taco. They're not too bad with a little dark brown gravy poured over them as well.*

2 pounds ground beef

½ large head cabbage, chopped

1 large onion, finely chopped

1 green bell pepper, seeded, finely chopped

2 to 3 garlic cloves, smashed, minced

Salt and freshly ground pepper to taste

2 11-ounce tubes bread dough (my mother used Pillsbury "French Loaf" oven bread dough)

Preheat oven to 350°F. In a large, deep skillet over medium-high heat, brown the ground beef until it is no longer pink. Add the cabbage, onion, green pepper and garlic. Add salt and pepper to taste. Cover and cook until the cabbage is wilted and the vegetables are tender. Drain the excess grease and cool to lukewarm.

Remove the bread dough from the tubes and cut into 6 equal portions. Using a rolling pin on a lightly floured board, roll out the dough sections into large squares or circles. They should be about ⅛-inch thick or slightly thinner and about 10 inches in diameter.

Place equal amounts of the beef mixture in the center of each portion of rolled out dough. Carefully fold the dough over the meat and form a packet, tucking the edges over and into one another to seal. Place the burger packets onto a greased cookie sheet and bake for 25 to 30 minutes. Serve with ketchup, relish or brown gravy.

# Beef and Vegetable Kebabs

MAKES 4 6-INCH KEBABS

*THESE ARE JUST PLAIN GOOD. I'm sure it's the marinade, with its little extra kick from the bourbon, and the sweetly oriental flavor it has. Dad's recipe calls for broiling them in the oven—he was never much of a barbecuer—but I think they are especially suited for the outdoor grill. The trick is to marinate them as long as you can before cooking them (I'd suggest injecting the beef cubes with the marinade, using the Cajun Injector sold on QVC).*

**MARINADE**

| | |
|---|---|
| ¼ | cup bourbon |
| ¼ | cup soy sauce |
| ¼ | cup Dijon-style mustard |
| ¼ | cup firmly packed brown sugar |
| 1 | small onion, finely minced or shredded |
| 1 | teaspoon salt |
| ⅓ | teaspoon freshly ground pepper or to taste |
| 2 | dashes Worcestershire sauce |

**KEBABS**

| | |
|---|---|
| 1½ | pounds sirloin, fillet or top round steak, cut into 1-inch cubes |
| 15 | to 20 white mushroom caps, about 1-inch in diameter |
| 3 | to 4 medium tomatoes, each cut into 5 to 6 wedges |
| 2 | green bell peppers, seeded, cut into 1-inch squares |
| 1 | large zucchini, cut into ¼-inch-thick rounds |
| 1 | 8-ounce can pineapple chunks, drained |
| 4 | 6-inch bamboo skewers or, if barbecuing, metal skewers |

**FOR MARINADE:** In a medium bowl, mix the first 8 ingredients. Place the meat cubes in the marinade. Turn several times to coat well. Cover and refrigerate at least 2 hours, preferably overnight.

**FOR KEBABS:** Remove the meat from the marinade. On each skewer, alternate the meat cubes and various vegetables and pineapple. Brush liberally with the marinade, then broil about 4 inches from the heat in the oven. Turn and baste frequently until done, about 12 minutes.

# Mom's Homemade BBQ Spareribs

MAKES 6 TO 8 SERVINGS

*MY MOM WAS A southern belle with a touch of Appalachian in her. She hailed from West Virginia, but her soul kept her looking toward Dixie. She mastered many great southern dishes, from fried chicken to these spareribs. Actually, I think Dad had something to do with the sauce, but he gave Mom all the credit. In my memory, I can still smell the house on the days she made these ribs—a thick, sweet, saucy scent I've not smelled since. You may come from the farthest northern corner of this country, but you'll speak with a drawl after your first bite.*

**RIBS**

- 3 to 4 slabs meaty ribs, cut into serving-size pieces
- 1 to 2 large onions, sliced into ¼-inch-thick rounds
- 3 to 4 large lemons, sliced into ¼-inch-thick rounds

**SAUCE**

- 1 cup ketchup
- ⅓ cup Worcestershire sauce
- 1 teaspoon chili powder
- 3 to 4 dashes hot pepper sauce (such as Tabasco)
- 2 cups water

**FOR RIBS:** Preheat the oven to 450°F. Place a slice of onion, topped with a slice of lemon, on the meaty side of each section of ribs — they should just about cover the section. Anchor with toothpicks. Place evenly in a roasting pan, meaty side up. Roast in oven for 30 minutes while making sauce.

**FOR SAUCE:** Place the ketchup, Worcestershire sauce, chili powder, hot pepper sauce and water in a saucepan and heat to boiling. Cook until it reduces a bit, turning thicker and saucier.

Pour the sauce evenly over the ribs in the roasting pan and return to the oven. Reduce the oven temperature to 350°F and roast until tender, about 45 to 60 minutes more, depending on thickness of ribs. Baste ribs with sauce every 12 to 15 minutes.

# Gilbert Hall Chili

MAKES 3 TO 4 QUARTS

*MY SISTER MAGGIE AND I went to the University of Delaware together. I was in Harrington Hall, she was in Gilbert Hall. She got the better deal, I think, because Gilbert Hall those years was blessed with some of the most natural cooks I've ever met. Their talents were especially revealed during exam weeks. During that crush of days at the end of every semester, the Gilbert Hall Gang, as they were called, kept a pot of chili cooking at all hours of the day or night, replenished by whoever took the last bowl. Over the four years, a recipe evolved that is sworn to by every one of us who sat bleary eyed over a bowl of it while flipping page after page of study notes. You may not have to pull an all-nighter these days, but you'll love this chili just the same (it's particularly good around 3:00 a.m. in the middle of winter).*

2 quarts tomato puree

2 3-ounce cans tomato paste

2 green bell peppers, chopped

½ large white or yellow onion, chopped

2 celery ribs, chopped

1 16-ounce can stewed tomatoes, cut up

8 tablespoons chili powder

⅓ 4½-ounce bottle Louisiana hot sauce or other hot sauce

1 teaspoon red wine vinegar

1 teaspoon garlic salt or to taste

3 pounds ground beef or ground turkey

4 15-ounce cans kidney beans, with juice

Chopped onion (optional)

Grated or shredded sharp Cheddar cheese (optional)

Place the first 10 ingredients in a large stockpot and simmer over medium-low to medium heat for about 2 hours.

About 15 minutes before the end of the simmer, brown the meat in a large skillet over high heat, until all the pink coloration is gone, and the meat is just beginning to brown. Add the meat and the kidney beans and their liquid to the chili pot and simmer another 30 minutes. Serve with chopped onions and/or grated cheese, if desired.

Main Courses

# Veal Marengo

*This is one of the newest cards in the Bowersox recipe file. It comes from Toni's Aunt Iris, who lives out in the great Northwest. It's a classic dish, Iris's favorite, and is quite easy to prepare. It's the mix of spices and juices that does it for me—that fresh explosion of flavors that would be a bright light if it were visual.*

½ cup vegetable oil

4 pounds veal shoulder, cut into 1-inch cubes

1 cup chopped onion

1 cup chopped celery

1 to 2 garlic cloves, crushed

1 cup dry white wine

2 16-ounce cans tomato sauce

1 bay leaf

1½ tablespoons chopped fresh oregano

¾ tablespoon chopped fresh rosemary

2 teaspoons salt

½ teaspoon freshly ground pepper

2 parsley sprigs

1 pound mushrooms, sliced

2 tablespoons lemon juice

¼ cup unsalted butter or margarine

1 tablespoon flour

Chopped fresh parsley for garnish

Heat the oil in a 6-quart Dutch oven over medium-high heat. Add half the veal cubes and cook until browned, then remove to a warm pan. Repeat with remaining veal and remove to the warmed pan when browned.

In the same pot, add the onion, celery and garlic, and cook until onion is wilted. Stir in ½ cup of the wine, the tomato sauce, bay leaf, oregano, rosemary, salt, pepper and parsley sprigs. Heat to boiling, then reduce heat to a simmer. Add the veal back in, cover, and simmer for about an hour and a half or until veal is tender. Remove the bay leaf.

Meanwhile, toss the mushrooms with the lemon juice. In a large skillet over medium-high heat, melt the butter, then add the mushrooms and sauté just until tender, about 3 minutes. Add the remaining ½ cup of wine and the mushrooms to the veal mixture. Dissolve the flour in 2 tablespoons of the pot liquid, then add to the pot, stirring until it is incorporated. Continue to simmer, uncovered, for another 15 minutes.

Put the Veal Marengo into a large serving dish, and sprinkle with the chopped parsley.

# Jalapeño Chicken

MAKES 4 SERVINGS

*My brother-in-law, Ken Morris, loves a little fire in his foods. Nothing crazy hot, now—just a little "authority," as my dad used to put it. Kenny also likes Southwestern cuisine, so when he came up with this recipe, it just made perfect sense. And while this is an exceptional chicken dish served warm, it makes a spectacular cold chicken salad the next day. Make sure you save some of the breast for the next day.*

2 teaspoons ground cinnamon

2 teaspoons chili powder

1 teaspoon ground cumin

1 tablespoon freshly ground pepper

2 teaspoons salt or to taste

1 3- to 4-pound frying chicken,
cut into serving pieces

1 cup chicken broth

2 tablespoons honey

Juice of 2 limes

1 teaspoon minced jalapeño pepper or,
for spicier chicken, use 1 tablespoon

Preheat oven to 450°F. In a small bowl, mix together the cinnamon, chili powder, cumin, pepper and salt. Rub this mixture into the chicken well (you can leave the skin on if you'd like, or remove it before rubbing in the powder).

Meanwhile, combine the chicken broth, honey, lime juice and jalapeño in a small saucepan. Cook over medium-high heat, uncovered, until the mixture is reduced to a syrupy texture. Remove from flame. The mixture will turn into a glaze.

Place the chicken in the oven, skin up. After the chicken has been cooking for 15 minutes, begin to baste every 10 minutes with the broth mixture. Cook for 45 minutes. Do not turn over, because the powdered skin will form a beautiful crust that is quite tasty. Serve immediately, or cool—makes a great tasting cold salad dish the next day.

# Chinese Cashew Chicken Casserole

MAKES ABOUT 6 SERVINGS

*RECIPES FOR CHICKEN CASSEROLES are legion. You can open almost any cookbook and find one. Ho-hum. But every once in a while, you'll come across the unusual, the quirky right turn someone has taken with a dish. This recipe is such a turn. What initially caught my eye was the use of tarragon, my favorite herb. Then I saw the Chinese angle, and the cashews. I was sold. I don't know where my sister and her husband came up with this, but I'm happy they did.*

1 to 2 tablespoons extra-virgin olive oil

2 pounds boneless skinless chicken (mix of white and dark meats), cut into 1-inch chunks

1 cup finely chopped celery

¼ cup finely chopped yellow onion

1 cup grated carrot

½ cup finely chopped green bell pepper

1 tablespoon chopped fresh tarragon or 1½ teaspoons dried

Salt and freshly ground pepper to taste

1 11-ounce can mushroom soup (undiluted)

½ cup chicken broth

1 5-ounce can Chinese noodles

1 cup whole and broken cashew nuts

In a large skillet or chicken fryer over medium-high heat, heat the olive oil, then add the chicken chunks and cook just until browned slightly. Using a slotted spoon, remove the chicken from the pan and place in a large bowl.

Add the celery, onion, carrot, green pepper and tarragon and gently toss to mix well. Season with salt and pepper to taste.

In a medium bowl, mix together the mushroom soup and chicken broth.

In a casserole dish large enough to hold the ingredients, place a layer of the Chinese noodles. Add half of the chicken mixture, then pour half of the soup and broth mix evenly over the top. Top this with another layer of the noodles, the rest of the chicken mixture and the rest of the soup and broth mix. Top with the cashews. Bake in a preheated 350°F oven for about 45 minutes.

# Nut-Crusted Chicken Breasts with Mustard Sauce

MAKES 4 SERVINGS

*THIS RECIPE COMES FROM my sister Maggie's files. I think she traded her Jezebel recipe (page 17) for it about 20 years ago. With so many of us eating more chicken for health reasons, it's nice to find a new recipe to stave off the boredom. And it's so simple to make. It will become one of your family's favorites the first time out.*

4 small to medium boneless skinless chicken breasts

5 tablespoons unsalted butter, melted

4 tablespoons Dijon-style mustard

½ cup finely chopped walnuts

Salt and freshly ground pepper to taste

½ cup plain yogurt

2 tablespoons mayonnaise

1 teaspoon honey

Chopped fresh parsley for garnish

Place each chicken breast between 2 pieces of wax paper and pound lightly with a wooden mallet or the back of a large serving spoon until about ¼- to ⅜-inch thick. Set aside.

In a bowl large enough to accommodate 1 of the breasts, whisk together the melted butter and 2 tablespoons of the mustard. Place the chopped walnuts in a second bowl of similar size. Dip each piece of chicken in the butter/mustard mix first, then in the walnuts. Coat the chicken well with the nuts. Place the chicken breasts in a shallow pan and sprinkle with a little salt and pepper to taste. Bake uncovered in a preheated 375°F oven for about 35 minutes or until cooked through without being dried out.

Just before serving, whisk together the yogurt, mayonnaise, remaining mustard and the honey in a small saucepan. Heat thoroughly, but don't boil. To serve the chicken, place a tablespoon of the sauce on each plate and swirl around. Place a chicken breast on the sauce, then drizzle with a bit more sauce. Sprinkle with parsley. Serve immediately.

# Hot Chicken Salad

MAKES 8 TO 10 SERVINGS

*HERE'S ONE OF MY MOTHER'S recipes that seems to work wherever you use it. It can be a light lunch, or the opening salvo in a multi-course evening; it can also be that staple that you make ahead and whip out for a quick dinner before running out to your evening activities. It can even dress up a brunch buffet beautifully. More than anything else, it's a terrific way to use that leftover roast chicken.*

| | |
|---|---|
| 2 | cups cooked rice |
| 2 to 3 | cups diced cooked chicken (white and dark meats) |
| 4 to 5 | hard-boiled eggs, chopped |
| 1 | small onion, chopped |
| 2 | tablespoons lemon juice |
| 1 | teaspoon salt |
| 1½ | cups chopped celery |
| 1 | cup sliced or coarsely chopped water chestnuts |
| ½ to ¾ | cup mayonnaise |
| 1 | 11-ounce can mushroom soup (undiluted) |
| 1½ | cups shredded Cheddar cheese |
| 1 to 2 | cups crushed potato chips |

Mix all ingredients except the cheese and the potato chips in a large bowl. Refrigerate overnight. Remove at least 1 hour before baking.

Combine the Cheddar and crushed potato chips in a small bowl.

Pour the contents of the large bowl into a casserole dish, and bake in a preheated 350°F oven for 30 to 40 minutes (depending on size and depth of casserole). About 10 minutes before the baking is finished, remove briefly from the oven and sprinkle the cheese and chips mixture over the top. Return to the oven for another 10 minutes or so, or until the top is hot and bubbly.

# Oven-Broiled Barbecue Chicken

MAKES 4 TO 6 SERVINGS

*THE SECRET HERE IS THE SAUCE. Anyone can broil chicken in the oven, but it took my dad a number of tries to perfect the sauce. He called it his "Chef's BBQ Sauce," and it's also great on steaks and pork chops as well. If you can't barbecue outside, try this inside. The sauce can be stored in the refrigerator for up to 2 weeks.*

**FOR SAUCE:** Combine all sauce ingredients and mix well. Let stand overnight, if possible, before using.

**FOR CHICKEN:** Baste or brush the sauce liberally over chicken breasts and legs, then place them on a broiling pan and broil for 20 minutes or until done. Turn and re-baste with sauce often while broiling, as this concentrates the flavor and helps retain moisture.

### SAUCE

- 1 cup Rhine wine
- ½ cup extra dry vermouth
- 1 cup olive oil
- 2 tablespoons steak sauce (such as A-1)
- 1 tablespoon dry mustard
- Juice of 1 lemon
- 2 medium onions, finely chopped
- 1 tablespoon salt
- 1 teaspoon freshly ground pepper
- ⅛ teaspoon thyme
- ⅛ teaspoon marjoram
- ⅛ teaspoon rosemary

### CHICKEN

- 4 chicken breasts, bone in, skin on or off, as desired
- 4 chicken legs, bone in, skin on or off, as desired

# Southwest Chicken Rolls

MAKES 4 SERVINGS

*I EXPLAINED MY BROTHER-IN-LAW Ken's penchant for Southwestern cuisine in a previous recipe. Well, as they say, the nut doesn't fall far from the tree. My nephew Zach, Ken's son, claims this as his favorite dish. While the blend of spices is certainly intriguing, it's the blend of cheeses rolled into the middle of the chicken that makes this a standout.*

4 boneless skinless chicken breasts

¼ cup shredded Cheddar cheese

¼ cup shredded Jalapeño cheese

1 3-ounce package cream cheese, softened

2 tablespoons unsalted butter or margarine, softened

2 tablespoons chopped green chilies

2 tablespoons grated onion

¼ teaspoon salt

⅛ teaspoon freshly ground pepper

1 cup crumbled Cheddar cheese crackers

1 teaspoon chili powder

¼ teaspoon ground cumin

¼ teaspoon ground red pepper

⅛ teaspoon garlic powder

¼ cup unsalted butter or margarine, melted

Place each chicken breast between 2 sheets of wax paper and pound to a ¼-inch thickness. Set aside.

Mix the Cheddar and Jalapeño cheeses together with the cream cheese, butter, green chilies, grated onion, salt and pepper. Make sure the mix is uniformly blended. Set aside.

In a medium to large bowl, crush the crackers and mix with the chili powder, cumin, red pepper and garlic powder. Set aside.

Place the chicken breasts on a flat work surface. Place equal amounts of the cheese mixture on each and spread over its surface. Roll each breast like a jelly roll, starting from the widest side. Secure the roll with a toothpick, or tie gently with string to hold it rolled. Dip each roll in the melted butter and then roll it gently in the cracker and herb mixture.

Bake uncovered in a preheated 400°F oven for 25 minutes. Serve hot.

# Toni's Peppers and Pasta

*My wife Toni is a courageous, creative cook. She's not afraid to try something on a whim, and doesn't mind the failures it takes to arrive at a success. This dish was a success from the first moment she tried it. She didn't want a heavy pasta sauce that night, and all we had were some peppers and garlic in the fridge. As it turned out, nothing more was needed. It's so simple to make, our daughter Taylor could make it, yet it eats like a $17.95 special. Enjoy.*

2 tablespoons extra-virgin olive oil

3 to 4 garlic cloves, minced

1 medium red bell pepper, seeded, julienned

1 medium yellow bell pepper, seeded, julienned

1 medium orange bell pepper, seeded, julienned

1 pound freshly made pasta (such as spaghetti, linguini or angel hair)

Salt and freshly ground pepper to taste

Freshly grated Parmesan or Romano cheese

In a large skillet or sauté pan over medium-high heat, warm the oil, then add the garlic and sauté for about 2 minutes or until the garlic has softened slightly. Add the peppers and toss to coat, then cook until they are crisp-tender or just a little softer (don't let them get real mushy).

While the peppers are sautéing, prepare the pasta. Freshly made pasta will cook to *al dente* in about 3 minutes in boiling salted water. Packaged pasta will require more time, so make sure you back-time the pasta so that you won't overcook the peppers while waiting for the pasta. Drain the pasta and place on individual serving plates. Top with equal amounts of the sautéed pepper mix. Season with salt and pepper. Serve immediately with the Parmesan cheese.

# Linguini with Sun-Dried Tomato Sauce

MAKES 4 TO 6 SERVINGS

*I DIDN'T DISCOVER SUN-DRIED TOMATOES until later in life. I regret that very much, because I love them unconditionally. There's something about that tangy, sweet pungency that is unmatched in nature. I started experimenting with them in a pasta sauce a few years ago, and this recipe is the result. It's become a staple dish at the Bowersox table, a hit every time it's served.*

| | |
|---|---|
| 3 | tablespoons olive oil |
| ½ | onion, chopped |
| 4 to 5 | garlic cloves, minced |
| 1 | pound Italian plum tomatoes, peeled, chopped |
| 8 to 12 | ounces sun-dried tomatoes, softened, chopped |
| ¾ | cup chicken stock |
| ¼ | teaspoon salt or to taste |
| ¼ | teaspoon freshly ground pepper or to taste |
| 3 | tablespoons chopped fresh basil |
| ½ | cup red wine |
| 1 to 1½ | pounds linguini or other heavier pasta such as spaghetti or fettucini |
| | Freshly grated Parmesan or Romano cheese |

Heat the olive oil in a large, deep skillet over medium-high heat until hot. Add the onion and sauté 30 seconds, then add the garlic. Sauté both until the onion is translucent. Add the tomatoes and stir, then the sun-dried tomatoes and stir again. Cover and simmer for about 2 minutes.

Add the chicken stock, salt, pepper and basil. Stir, cover and simmer another 2 to 3 minutes. Add the wine, stir and simmer uncovered for about 3 minutes. If the sauce appears to be drying out a little, add a touch more wine, stir and lower the heat.

Meanwhile, cook the pasta according to package directions. If it's freshly made pasta (recommended), cook it about 3 minutes in boiling, salted water (to *al dente*).

Drain the pasta and place in servings on plates. Ladle a generous amount of the sauce over the pasta. Serve with the grated cheese.

# Don's Homemade Pasta Sauce

*DAD WAS REALLY PROUD of this sauce. He spent years perfecting it, never quite satisfied with each new batch. I think that if he were alive, he'd still be tweaking it today. But once he got the basics of the sauce, he went to work on the meatballs, and those were the crowning glory. I put a range of garlic cloves in the recipe, but Dad often added a dozen cloves (God bless him!). Use your own judgement, but regardless of your choice, I think you'll find the sauce beats any jarred sauce you can find.*

**FOR SAUCE:** In a large skillet over medium to medium-high heat, sauté the onions and garlic in the olive oil until translucent. Set aside.

In a large, nonreactive stockpot over medium heat, simmer the tomato puree, tomato paste, water, Italian seasoning and sugar. When well blended and warmed, add the onion and garlic mixture. Cover and simmer at least an hour.

**FOR MEATBALLS:** Combine all the ingredients in a large bowl and mix thoroughly by hand, taking care not to over-knead the meat, or the meatballs will be too tight and hard. Form the meat mixture into 1½-inch meatballs. You should be able to get between 10 and 12 of them. Add the meatballs to the sauce, cover and simmer another hour or more. Serve with any pasta.

## SAUCE

- 3 tablespoons extra-virgin olive oil
- 4 large onions, chopped
- 4 to 6 garlic cloves, minced
- 2 28-ounce cans tomato puree
- 1 18-ounce can tomato paste
- 1 28-ounce can water
- ½ teaspoon Italian seasoning
- 1 teaspoon sugar

## MEATBALLS

- ½ pound ground beef
- ½ pound ground veal
- ½ pound ground pork
- 2 eggs
- 2 garlic cloves, chopped
- 3 tablespoons grated Parmesan cheese
- ½ teaspoon oregano
- 1¼ teaspoons salt or to taste
- 3 tablespoons chopped fresh parsley
- 1 teaspoon lemon juice

# Garden Lasagne

*THIS NICE TWIST ON an old standby was offered to our family by Mrs. Chrone, the Italian mother of my best friend during my early teen years in Westfield, New Jersey. Dad was always pestering Mrs. Chrone to share her Old World secrets, so she offered him this lasagne. It's terrific in late summer, with the enormous variety of fresh vegetables in the markets then. Feel free to substitute any vegetable that fits your taste.*

**SAUCE**

| | |
|---|---|
| 1½ | cups sliced mushrooms |
| 1 | cup chopped celery |
| ½ | cup chopped green pepper |
| ½ | cup chopped onion |
| 2 | garlic cloves, minced |
| 3 | tablespoons olive oil |
| 1 | 12-ounce can Italian plum tomatoes |
| 1 | 8-ounce can tomato sauce |
| 1 | 6-ounce can tomato paste |
| 2 | tablespoons minced fresh parsley |
| 1 | teaspoon Italian seasoning |
| | Salt and freshly ground pepper to taste |
| 1½ | cups water |
| 2 | cups sliced zucchini |

**LASAGNE**

| | |
|---|---|
| 12 | ounces lasagne noodles |
| 1 | pound ricotta cheese |
| 1 | egg (optional) |
| 1 | 10-ounce package chopped frozen spinach, thawed, drained |
| 1½ | cups shredded Cheddar cheese |
| ½ | cup grated Parmesan cheese |

**FOR SAUCE:** Sauté the mushrooms, celery, green pepper, onion and garlic in the oil for about 5 minutes in a large stockpot. Add the tomatoes, the tomato sauce, tomato paste, seasonings and 1 cup of the water. Simmer, covered, for about 1 hour. Add the remaining water and simmer 15 minutes longer. When the sauce is finished simmering, add the zucchini. Sauce can be made ahead.

**FOR LASAGNE:** Cook the noodles in boiling salted water. While cooking, mix together the ricotta, egg (if using) and spinach.

Grease a 9 x 13-inch baking dish and layer ingredients as follows: On the bottom, put ⅓ of the noodles, cover with ⅓ of the sauce, ½ of the ricotta-spinach mix, and ⅓ of the Cheddar. Repeat layers. Top with the remaining noodles and sauce. Sprinkle with remaining Cheddar and all of the Parmesan. Bake in a preheated 350°F oven for 45 to 60 minutes, or until bubbly and slightly browned around the edges.

# Don's Pesto Spaghetti

*I THINK MY FATHER was fascinated with Italy, Italians and Italian cuisine. He was always dabbling with sauces and breads, cannolis, pastas and the like. He was overjoyed when I told him I was marrying Toni, who is part Italian. During his winemaking phase, he was always trying to master chianti. When he talked, he used his hands a lot. The rest of the family, of course, benefitted from his infatuation with all things Italian, because we got to savor creations like this pasta, the heart of which is a masterful pesto.*

**DON'S PESTO SAUCE**

- 4 to 6 garlic cloves
- 1 teaspoon salt
- 2 cups fresh basil leaves (pack firmly into measuring cup)
- 2 tablespoons pine nuts
- ½ cup extra-virgin olive oil
- ½ cup grated Parmesan cheese
- ¼ cup grated Romano cheese
- 4 tablespoons unsalted butter, softened
- Water, as needed

**SPAGHETTI**

- 8 ounces spaghetti, linguini or capellini
- 1 to 2 tablespoons unsalted butter
- 1 onion, chopped
- 10 to 12 white mushrooms, sliced
- Freshly grated Parmesan cheese to taste or mixture of Asiago, Reggiano and Pecorino cheeses

**FOR SAUCE:** In a food processor or blender, put the garlic, salt, basil, pine nuts and olive oil and process until smooth. Add the cheeses and butter and process very briefly, just to incorporate them. Add hot water a tablespoon at a time if you need to thin the pesto a little—process briefly after adding each bit of water.

**FOR SPAGHETTI:** Cook the spaghetti until *al dente* (about 8 minutes for dried, packaged pasta, about 3 minutes for freshly made pasta). Drain when ready to mix with sauce.

While pasta is cooking, sauté the chopped onion in the butter. When the onions are translucent, add the mushrooms. Heat the pesto sauce in a small saucepan.

Drain the pasta and place in a large serving bowl. Add in the onions and mushrooms and the pesto sauce. Toss well to coat and mix. Top with the grated cheese and serve.

# Mrs. C's Eggplant Parmagiano

MAKES 6 SERVINGS

*I HAVE TO TELL YOU—I have no idea who Mrs. C—Mrs. Crescenzo—is. Perhaps Mom and Dad knew her from church or the PTA. What I do know is that this recipe turned up in my father's private recipe file, and nothing got in there unless it was spectacular. Upon trying it, I can see why he granted it entrance into his personal Valhalla. Mrs. Crescenzo, who-ever you may be—thank you!*

1½  cups milk

2  eggs, beaten

1  medium eggplant, peeled, sliced into ¼- to ½-inch slices

Seasoned Italian breadcrumbs

Flour for coating

Olive oil for shallow frying

Garlic salt to taste

Onion salt to taste

2  to 3 15-ounce cans tomato sauce or Dad's homemade (page 57)

Freshly grated Romano or Parmesan cheese

1  ball mozzarella cheese, cut into ⅛-inch-thick slices

Dried oregano

Blend the milk and eggs in a small bowl. Dip the eggplant slices into the milk mixture, then into a bowl of the breadcrumbs, then into a bowl of flour. Heat the olive oil in a high-sided skillet or sauté pan over medium heat (the oil should only be about ¼-inch deep, if that). Fry the eggplant until golden, flipping to ensure both sides are done. Remove from the oil, and drain on paper towels. While draining, sprinkle with the garlic salt and onion salt to taste.

Pour about ⅓ of the tomato sauce into the bottom of a 9 x 13-inch ovenproof glass baking dish. Place about ⅓ of the eggplant slices overlapping each other slightly on the bottom of the dish. Sprinkle liberally with the Romano. Place slices of mozzarella on top of the eggplant and cheese. Pour another ⅓ of the sauce over the top of all of this. Repeat the layers again, ending with the sauce on top, sprinkled with a bit of the cheese and oregano.

Bake in a preheated 350°F oven for 20 to 30 minutes, or until the cheese has melted throughout. Serve hot with Romano on the side.

# Iris's Vegetarian Pizza

MAKES 1 LARGE (12-INCH) PIZZA

*IRIS IS TONI'S AUNT, though you'd never peg her for that. She looks more like her sister— beautiful, youthful, vivacious. She's a wicked Scrabble player too. Though she's not a vegetarian, she passed along this recipe when we told her we had a yen for pizza but weren't interested in all the greasy meats and cheeses you usually get with pizza parlor pizzas. We loved it instantly. It takes a little extra effort, but it's certainly worth it, especially if you've been dying for a pizza, but want to keep the diet intact.*

2   garlic bulbs, unpeeled

3   tablespoons olive oil

1   large red onion, cut into thick rings

⅓   cup oil-packed sun-dried tomatoes, drained, oil reserved

1   large pizza crust, thrown or rolled out, placed on pizza pan

2   cups grated mozzarella cheese

½   cup roasted red peppers (jar type), cut into ½-inch-thick strips

⅔   cup crumbled feta cheese (about 2½ ounces)

4   tablespoons chopped fresh basil

2   tablespoons chopped fresh parsley

Preheat the oven to 375°F. Slice off the top of the garlic bulbs and place them in a small baking dish and drizzle with a tablespoon of olive oil. Wipe a baking or cookie sheet with a tablespoon of olive oil and place the onion rings on the sheet. Drizzle them with a little olive oil. Bake both the garlic and the onion rings together for about 30 minutes. Remove and cool.

Squeeze out the baked garlic into the bowl of a food processor or blender. Add the sun-dried tomatoes and pulse until smooth. Add just enough oil to make a smooth, spreadable paste.

Preheat the oven to 450°F. Spread the garlic-tomato paste over the crust. Top with the mozzarella cheese, the onion, the peppers and the feta. Sprinkle with 2 tablespoons of the basil and 1 tablespoon of the parsley. Bake for 20 minutes or until crust is golden brown and cheese is bubbly. Cool 5 minutes, then sprinkle with remaining basil and parsley. Cut and serve.

# Coquilles St. Jacques Crepes

MAKES 4 TO 5 SERVINGS

*THIS WAS ONE OF THE MOST ordered dishes in my restaurant, The Crepe Chalet. We made it with sea scallops (the big ones) but it can also be made with the smaller bay scallops (which is probably more traditional). And while this recipe calls for crepes, the coquilles can also be served in individual scallop dishes as an appetizer or entrée dish, in which case you'd set the dishes in the oven and bake them until the cheeses melt (I'd also top them with a little Parmesan cheese as well).*

## CREPES

- 4 eggs
- ½ cup milk
- ½ teaspoon salt
- ½ cup chicken stock
- 1 tablespoon unsalted butter or margarine, melted
- 1 cup flour

## COQUILLES

- ⅓ cup dry white wine
- 2 tablespoons chopped green onions
- 1 cup sliced white mushrooms
- 1 to 1½ pounds sea scallops, cut into ¼- to ½-inch pieces
- 3 tablespoons unsalted butter
- 3 tablespoons flour
- ½ teaspoon salt
- 1½ cups light cream or evaporated milk
- 2 tablespoons chopped fresh parsley
- 8 to 10 cooked crepes
- ½ cup grated Swiss cheese

**FOR CREPES:** Make the crepes by combining all the ingredients except the flour in a bowl and beating together. Gradually add the flour and whisk or beat until a smooth batter is achieved. Drop a small ladleful of batter into a small frying pan or crepe pan that has been preheated. Swirl the batter quickly as you pour it into the pan, so it coats the pan with a very thin layer of batter. The crepe will let go of the pan around the edges when it is time to flip it—don't overcook, or they'll burn. Heat the flip side only about 20 seconds. Place on a plate between layers of wax paper until needed.

**FOR COQUILLES:** Combine the white wine, green onions, mushrooms and scallops in a nonstick saucepan and simmer for 5 minutes.

While doing this, melt the butter in a large skillet and stir in the flour and salt to make a roux (a caramel-colored mixture). Pour in the cream and cook until a creamy thick sauce is achieved—stir this constantly while doing. Add the parsley and then the scallop mixture.

Fill each crepe with 3 to 4 tablespoons of the scallop mixture (or whatever amount will cover the center third of each crepe). Fold the other two thirds of the crepe over the center and sprinkle with the cheese. Place in a preheated 350°F oven for about 10 minutes, or until the cheese melts.

# Tuna Soufflé

MAKES A 1½-QUART CASSEROLE

*HERE'S A RECIPE that seemed to be way ahead of its time. Mom used to make it with canned tuna, and while we kids loved it, the recipe really didn't come into its own until I met and married Toni years later. Her uncle Johnny was a sport fisherman, and would stop by every once in a while with pretty much a whole yellow fin tuna he'd caught. After eating all the grilled tuna steaks we could handle, this recipe came in handy for leftover tuna or pieces too small to grill. Whether you use fresh or canned tuna, this is a light and tasty way to enjoy it.*

6 to 8 slices bread, crusts removed, cut into cubes

7 to 10 ounces fresh tuna, cooked, or canned tuna

¼ pound Cheddar cheese, grated

3 eggs, beaten

1 teaspoon salt or to taste

⅓ teaspoon white pepper

2 cups milk

Cover the bottom of a 1½-quart casserole dish with a layer of bread cubes. Crumble the tuna (drain the liquid first if using canned) and flake it evenly across the top of the bread cubes. Top that with the cheese and a final layer of bread cubes.

Add the eggs, salt and pepper to the milk and blend well. Pour this mixture evenly over the bread, cheese and tuna.

Bake in a preheated 325°F oven for about 1 hour.

# Salmon Rolls with Horseradish-Dill Stuffing

*I DON'T KNOW WHAT got me started on this recipe. But I've always liked horseradish with salmon, and dill with salmon, and I'm a big fan of stuffing. Natural evolution took over from there, I suppose. This is a little labor intensive, but it's well worth the effort, I guarantee you.*

½ cup finely crumbled fresh breadcrumbs

1 tablespoon minced yellow onion

¼ cup minced dill pickle gherkins

¾ tablespoon minced fresh sage or
   ¾ teaspoon dried

1 teaspoon minced fresh thyme or
   ½ teaspoon dried

   Salt and freshly ground pepper to taste

2½ tablespoons unsalted butter, melted

¼ to ⅓ cup prepared horseradish

¼ cup light cream or milk

   Dill pickle juice

1 1-pound salmon fillet (about ¾-inch
   thick at center), skin removed, sliced
   horizontally to ¼-inch thickness

3 tablespoons unsalted butter, melted

   Thinly sliced baby dill gherkins and
   fresh dill sprigs for garnish

Prepare the stuffing by combining the bread-crumbs, onion, pickle and herbs in a bowl. Season to taste with salt and pepper. Mix thoroughly, then add the butter, horseradish, cream and enough of the dill pickle juice to achieve a moist (though not "wet") stuffing mixture. Set aside. Preheat the oven to 375°F.

Lay the salmon pieces flat on your work surface. Season with a little salt and pepper. Carefully place a layer of the stuffing mixture across the entire surface of the fillet pieces. It should be about ⅛-inch thick. Then roll up each piece jelly roll fashion, and secure by tying at either end with light cotton string.

Place the rolls in a baking dish with about ¼ cup water in the bottom. Drizzle melted butter over the rolls, then cover and bake until salmon is opaque, about 25 to 30 minutes. Remove from the oven, discard the string and serve with the garnishes. Serve as a complete roll, or carefully slice medallions ½-inch thick and arrange them on the plate.

# Individual Shrimp and Zucchini Casseroles

MAKES 6 SERVINGS

*THESE INDIVIDUAL CASSEROLES make terrific first courses. Two of them on a plate with a vegetable can also serve well as an entrée. What I've always liked about them was that you can spice each one up individually—add some garlic to one, a little hot pepper to another, or tarragon to a third. It's up to you. And if you put them in the fridge after you've baked them, they chill nicely into little molds that look great on a bed of lettuce for a light lunch.*

Butter or nonstick cooking spray

4 cups shredded zucchini (about 2 to 3 large or 1½ pounds)

1½ cups shredded Swiss cheese (about 6 ounces)

1 pound small to medium shrimp, peeled, deveined

4 eggs

1⅓ cups milk

½ teaspoon salt

⅛ teaspoon white pepper

½ teaspoon tarragon

Butter (or spray with nonstick cooking spray) 6 10-ounce individual casseroles—you can also use heavy ceramic soup ramekins as well. Press ⅔ cup of shredded zucchini on the bottom and around the sides of each casserole. Put ¼ cup of the cheese in the center of each. Divide the shrimp among the casseroles, reserving 6 to use as garnish toppers. Place them on top of the cheese, arranged evenly in the casserole space.

Cook the shrimp for garnish in salted boiling water for 4 minutes. Drain and set aside.

Lightly beat the eggs, milk, salt, pepper and tarragon together in a small bowl, then pour the mixture over the shrimp in the casseroles. Bake in a preheated 400°F oven for 15 minutes, then reduce the heat to 350°F and bake for 20 minutes or until the custard is set in each casserole.

# Shrimp and Potato Gumbo

MAKES 10 8-OUNCE SERVINGS

*HERE'S A GREAT RECIPE from my cousin Sue and her husband Ron, who live in the heart of Cajun country in Louisiana. As Sue, a born and bred Northerner, told me, "This was one of the biggest and most pleasant surprises to me in Cajun food." Most people think of Cajun as hot and spicy, but it's really all about fresh, flavorful ingredients. This gumbo is a perfect example.*

1 cup (2 sticks) unsalted butter or margarine

1 cup flour

1 medium onion, very finely chopped

2 to 3 celery ribs, very finely chopped

2 to 3 garlic cloves, minced

2 tablespoons chopped fresh parsley

3 to 5 green onions (white and green parts), finely chopped

½ green bell pepper, chopped (optional)

Water (about 4 cups)

Salt and freshly ground pepper to taste

2 to 3 baking potatoes (depends on how much potato you want to balance with the shrimp), peeled, cubed

1 to 1½ pounds medium to large shrimp, peeled, deveined

Hot cooked white rice

In a large stockpot, make a roux by cooking the butter and flour together over low heat. Cook until the roux is the color of a copper penny, stirring often.

Add the onion, celery, garlic, parsley, green onions and green pepper (if using) to the roux, cooking on low heat and stirring often so it doesn't burn. Cook until the onions are translucent.

Add enough water to make the mixture slightly more runny than you want your stew to end up, as it will thicken while you cook it. Add salt and pepper to taste. Cover and cook for at least 2 hours on low heat to maximize the flavors.

Add the potatoes to the stew and continue cooking until they are tender, about ½ hour. Then add the shrimp and cook for another 15 minutes until they cook through and turn coral. Serve the stew in a bowl over hot, cooked white rice.

Main Courses

# Sautéed Scallops with Garlic-Balsamic Glaze

MAKES 2 SERVINGS

*ONE OF OUR FAVORITE RESTAURANTS is the Dilworthtown Inn near Chadd's Ford, Pennsylvania. They serve a scallop appetizer that is out of this world. After many attempts to duplicate the salty-sweet crust they get on their scallops, I ended up with this recipe. I suppose the evolution was inevitable, given my love of both balsamic vinegar and garlic. Oh well—now I have two favorite scallop dishes.*

2 tablespoons olive oil

2 to 3 garlic cloves, smashed, minced

1 pound large sea scallops, rinsed, drained

Salt and freshly ground pepper to taste

¼ teaspoon cayenne pepper

¼ cup balsamic vinegar

2 tablespoons unsalted butter

1 to 2 tablespoons chopped fresh coriander

Heat a large nonstick skillet over medium-high heat until hot. Add the olive oil, then the garlic and sauté until the garlic is just beginning to wilt. Quickly add the scallops 1 at a time. Watch them carefully, as they'll cook very fast and you don't want to overcook them. Turn them over 1 at a time as they brown (no more than 2 minutes a side). Sprinkle with a little salt, pepper and cayenne as they brown. Remove them to a slightly warm plate as they finish and keep warm.

Add the balsamic vinegar to whatever liquid is still in the pan and cook over the same medium-high heat until it is reduced to a glaze, about 5 minutes. Swirl in the butter until dissolved. Return the scallops to the pan and add the coriander. Using a spoon, coat each scallop with the sauce as they reheat.

To serve, spread a tablespoon or 2 of the sauce on the serving plate, then set an equal amount of the scallops in the center of the sauce. Drizzle a little of any remaining sauce on each scallop and serve immediately.

# Granny's Crab Cakes

MAKES ABOUT 10 CAKES

*WHILE THESE ARE CONSIDERED the finest crab cakes in existence by those who have tried them, they didn't start out as crab cakes at all. Actually, back in the 1930s, Granny's mother (Toni's great-grandmother) started making salmon cakes for her neighbors in the Polish neighborhood of Wilmington, Delaware, where Granny grew up. They became so popular that Great-Granny began selling the salmon cakes to anyone who wanted them. She had quite a business going after a couple of years. When Granny started her own family, crab was easier to get in the neighborhood than salmon, so the salmon cakes became crab cakes. A fortuitous switch, as the recipe lent itself even better to crab. Just try one. You'll see.*

| | |
|---|---|
| 4 | slices white bread |
| 3 | to 4 heaping tablespoons unsalted butter or margarine |
| 2 | medium carrots, finely shredded |
| 1½ | onions, finely chopped |
| 1 | large green pepper, finely chopped |
| ½ | teaspoon salt |
| ¼ | teaspoon freshly ground pepper |
| | Hot pepper sauce (such as Tabasco) to taste |
| 1 | egg, lightly beaten |
| 1 | pound fresh crabmeat, drained, picked over |
| 1 | 15-ounce can breadcrumbs |
| | Vegetable oil |

On a large cookie sheet or baking sheet, lay out the bread and sprinkle it with water until it is damp, then gently press out the water (you can do this by putting the pieces on a stack of 2 to 3 paper towels).

Melt the butter in a large skillet. Sauté the carrots in the butter for about 2 to 3 minutes. Then add the onions and sauté another 1 to 2 minutes. Then add the green pepper and sauté for 1 to 2 minutes. Remove the pan from the heat and mix in the salt and pepper. Add in the hot pepper sauce desired (I usually add 8 to 10 drops, but I like the cakes spicy).

Pour the vegetable mixture into a large bowl. Add in the egg and gently blend it into the mixture. Gently tear the bread slices into small pieces and toss them into the bowl, then add the crab. Using your hands, gently mix all the ingredients together, so they are blended evenly, but not crushed and matted into lumps or so the crab is broken down.

Form the crab mixture into cakes — you don't want them too fat, they should be 2½- to 3-inches across. Make sure they hold together, then, holding them in your hand, generously sprinkle them with breadcrumbs. Make sure you get the sides well coated as the tops and bottoms.

You can individually wrap the cakes at this point and freeze them, or you can cook them right away. Fry them in a little oil in a skillet over medium-high heat, or bake them in a preheated 350°F oven for about 20 minutes, or broil them until they are browned and cooked through. Serve with tartar sauce, ketchup or seafood sauce.

Here I am with Granny at our annual Christmas party, which featured these crab cakes

# SIDE DISHES

Green Beans with Herb Sauce

Mushroom Turnovers

Italian Zucchini Pie

Ten-Layer Salad

Marinated Mixed Vegetables

Crepe Chalet Caesar Salad

Mrs. B's Never-Fail Cheese Soufflé

Granny's Cole Slaw

Beef, Mushroom and Rice Stuffed Squash

Hot Crabmeat and Avocado Salad

Zesty Green Rice

Tahini Salad Dressing

Potato Casserole

Sourdough Cheese Bread

Minted Fruit and Rice Salad

Tuscan Bread

Asian Shrimp and Spinach Salad

Granny's Polish Easter Bread

Jeanne's Scones

# Green Beans with Herb Sauce

*I've NEVER BEEN A FAN of vegetables nature's way—naked. Undressed broccoli or spinach, brussels sprouts or beans just don't do it for me. It's not that I don't like them; it's just that it's so easy to dress them up, to give them a little punch, a little panache, a little personality.*

*Like these beans—no effort, but a lot of style.*

- 1 pound green beans, trimmed
- ¼ cup unsalted butter or margarine
- ¾ cup minced onion
- 1 garlic clove, minced
- ¼ cup minced celery
- ¼ cup chopped fresh parsley
- ¼ teaspoon rosemary
- ¼ teaspoon basil
- ¾ teaspoon salt or to taste

Steam or cook the green beans in a large saucepan until fork-tender. Set aside on low heat.

In a second saucepan over medium-high heat, melt the butter and sauté the onion, garlic and celery for 5 minutes. Add the herbs and salt and simmer for another 5 to 7 minutes.

Just before serving, toss the beans with the sauce to cover well.

# Mushroom Turnovers

MAKES 12 TURNOVERS

*WHAT MAKES THESE so enticing is their versatility. I present these as a single vegetable side dish, but the truth is, they can be whatever you want them to be. You can add chopped shrimp and stir-fry vegetables to them, or flaked crab, or diced chicken and broccoli. The possibilities are endless.*

**PASTRY**

- 1 8-ounce package cream cheese
- ½ pound (2 sticks) unsalted butter
- ¼ teaspoon salt
- 2¼ cups flour

**FILLING**

- 3 tablespoons unsalted butter
- 1 large onion, finely chopped
- ½ pound fresh mushrooms (mix of white, shiitake, crimini, portobello), sliced
- ¼ teaspoon thyme
- ½ teaspoon salt or to taste
- ½ teaspoon freshly ground pepper
- 2 tablespoons flour
- ¼ cup sour cream
- 1 egg, beaten, mixed with about 1 tablespoon water

*F*OR PASTRY: Knead together all ingredients into a dough, then roll into a ball. Wrap in waxed paper and chill for 4 hours before using.

FOR FILLING: Melt the butter in a skillet over medium heat and cook the onions until evenly browned. Add mushrooms and cook about 3 minutes. Add thyme, salt and pepper and stir to blend. Sprinkle the flour over the top of mushroom mixture, then stir in sour cream, stir again, and cook until thickened.

While mushroom mixture is cooking, roll out the dough on a lightly floured surface to about an ⅛-inch thickness. Cut into 4-inch rounds. Place some of filling into each—too little and the turnovers will seem doughy, too much and they'll pop open. Fold the dough circle over filling, lightly brush edge with the beaten egg wash and press edges together (gently use the tines of a fork). Poke tines of the fork through top of each turnover to let out steam when they are cooking. The turnovers can be frozen at this point.

To bake, brush each with a little of the egg wash and bake in a preheated 325°F oven for 30 minutes or until browned.

77

# Italian Zucchini Pie

*I'M SURE THIS WAS another one of those recipes that Dad collected from his Italian friends and acquaintances. He immediately would have been intrigued by the mix of cheeses (cheese was high on his list of God's true gifts to Man) and he would have liked the idea of using his pie dough recipe in a casserole (we Bowersoxes are always experimenting). It's a great recipe, perfect as an unusual side dish, but it makes a nice vegetable entrée as well.*

4 cups thinly sliced zucchini

1 cup chopped onion

½ cup (1 stick) unsalted butter or margarine or ¼ cup extra-virgin olive oil

½ cup chopped fresh parsley or 2 tablespoons dried flakes

½ teaspoon salt

½ teaspoon freshly ground pepper

¼ teaspoon garlic powder

¼ teaspoon chopped fresh basil

¼ teaspoon chopped fresh oregano

2 eggs, beaten

2 cups shredded mozzarella cheese or Muenster

1 tablespoon Dijon-style mustard

1 homemade pie crust (to fit inside 10-inch-round casserole) or 2 to 3 8-ounce rolls Pillsbury croissant dough

In a large skillet or sauté pan, sauté the zucchini and onion in the butter until zucchini is softened and onions are translucent. Stir in the chopped parsley, salt, pepper, garlic powder, basil and oregano.

In a large mixing bowl, combine the eggs, cheese and mustard, then add the zucchini/onion mixture.

Spread the pie crust across the bottom and up the sides of a casserole dish or baking dish that has been lightly greased. If using the croissant dough, roll it out on a lightly floured surface and roll to pie crust thickness. Carefully lift it into the dish and press across the bottom and up the sides.

Pour zucchini mixture into the crust and bake in a preheated 375°F oven for 18 to 20 minutes. Cover with foil for last 10 minutes of baking. Let stand 10 minutes before serving.

# Marinated Mixed Vegetables

MAKES 6 SERVINGS

*While my sister Maggie was a designer for Aspen Skiwear and OP a number of years ago, she had the good fortune of working with a young fashion designer she called only Kiyo. Kiyo was Japanese, and over the years, Maggie collected many recipes from her that have become favorites in her family. If you like the mix of sweet and sour in Japanese cooking, you'll love this dish as much as we do.*

## VEGETABLES

- 1 cup broccoli florets
- ½ cup cauliflower florets
- ½ cup yellow squash, cut into ¼-inch-thick half-rounds
- 1 medium carrot, cut into ⅛-inch-thick rounds or on diagonal
- ½ red bell pepper, julienned
- ½ yellow bell pepper, julienned

## MARINADE

- 2 tablespoons sugar
- 1 tablespoon red wine vinegar or cider vinegar
- 1 tablespoon canola oil
- 1 tablespoon sake
- ½ teaspoon minced garlic
- 1 tablespoon minced onion
- ¼ teaspoon oregano

**FOR VEGETABLES:** Prepare all the vegetables and place them in a shallow bowl or casserole dish.

**FOR MARINADE:** In a small bowl mix together the sugar, vinegar, oil, sake, garlic, onion and oregano. Pour the marinade over the vegetables and let stand in refrigerator overnight.

To cook the vegetables, you can either place them in a steamer and add a little of the marinade to the steaming water, or place them in a large saucepan with a little water and a tablespoon or 2 of the marinade and cook them until the vegetables are fork-tender and bright in color.

# Mrs. B's Never-Fail Cheese Soufflé

MAKES 4 SERVINGS

*I DON'T KNOW IF THERE'S anything quite as tricky as a soufflé. They're delicate, petulant little things that require patience and a high tolerance for frustration. Mom never worried about them though—she was so successful with this one that her reputation with it became the name. It's a light, airy beauty, tangy with the flavor of cheese, that just about melts in your mouth.*

- 4 tablespoons flour
- ¼ teaspoon salt
- Dash freshly ground pepper
- ½ cup mayonnaise
- 4 tablespoons milk
- 1 cup grated cheese (such as Cheddar, Swiss or Monterey Jack)
- 4 egg whites
- Dash cream of tartar

Grease a soufflé dish and make a collar of aluminum foil around the top. This will keep the edges from burning and baking onto the dish, which makes it hard to remove the soufflé.

In a mixing bowl, gently stir the flour, salt and pepper into the mayonnaise. Don't overmix. Add milk slowly, stirring until smooth. Stir in the cheese gently, but thoroughly.

Beat the egg whites until stiff. Add in the cream of tartar while beating. Gently fold the mayonnaise mixture and the egg whites together until blended (don't overdo it). Pour into the soufflé dish and bake in a preheated 325°F oven for 60 minutes. Cool a minute or 2 before serving.

# Beef, Mushroom and Rice Stuffed Squash

MAKES 4 MAIN COURSE SERVINGS OR 8 SIDE SERVINGS

*My sister Maggie and her husband Ken are great ones for playing around with a recipe. They like to experiment. Which is fine by me, because whenever they go into their "lab," they come out with spectacular results. Witness this recipe for jazzing up the lowly squash.*

½   cup chopped onion

½   cup chopped celery

1   garlic clove, crushed

2   tablespoons vegetable oil

1   pound ground beef or ground turkey

1   cup chopped peeled tomatoes

1   cup sliced fresh mushrooms

¾   cup cooked white or brown rice

2   tablespoons chopped fresh flatleaf parsley

1   tablespoon chopped fresh basil or 1 teaspoon dried

1   teaspoon salt

½   teaspoon freshly ground pepper

3   to 4 yellow squash or green zucchini

½   cup grated Parmesan cheese

In a large skillet over medium-high heat, sauté the onion, celery and garlic in the oil until golden. Remove to a warm bowl or second pan, and put the meat in the same skillet and sauté until brown, breaking it up as needed.

Stir in the tomatoes and mushrooms, the rice and the seasonings, and cook until hot. Add back in the onion mixture and combine. Set aside the stuffing in a warm bowl.

To prepare the squash, cut in half lengthwise and blanch in salted, boiling water for 3 to 5 minutes. Remove carefully and set on a flat work surface. Using a teaspoon or melon baller, scrape out the seeds and pulp. Make sure you don't puncture the outer skin. Leave about ⅛-inch walls. Place the stuffing into the squash shells. Don't overpack them so the stuffing is hard and tight. Mound it a little, as it will settle slightly when baking. Put the shells in a baking dish or open casserole dish and bake in a preheated 350°F oven for about 20 minutes. For the last 5 minutes, top with the Parmesan cheese, so it melts into the stuffing a little.

# Zesty Green Rice

MAKES 4 SERVINGS

*I FOUND THIS RECIPE tucked in the back of the family recipe box. It's in my mother's hand-writing, quite obviously quickly scrawled on a small piece of notepaper, something she probably jotted down during an after-church conversation or while chatting on the phone with a friend. I don't remember her ever making this dish, but being a lover of rice, I decided to try it as I was putting this book together. Wherever Mom got the recipe, I'm glad she kept it. It's a wonderfully tangy twist to a basic side dish.*

**RICE**

- 2 cups rice
- 2 cups chicken broth

**SAUCE**

- 1 pint sour cream
- 1 tablespoon mashed (to paste) anchovies
- 4 green onions (white and green parts), minced
- 1 tablespoon red wine vinegar
- ¼ cup chopped fresh parsley
- Salt and freshly ground pepper to taste

**F**OR RICE: Cook the rice in the chicken broth as per package directions.

**FOR SAUCE:** In a mixing bowl, place the first five ingredients for the sauce and stir to blend well. Season with salt and pepper to taste.

Serve the rice as a side dish, topped with a large dollop of the sauce.

*My mom, about 25 years old, at her family home in West Virginia*

# Potato Casserole

*Scalloped potatoes was a staple in my mom's house. It was one of her signature dishes, and on the table one or two nights a week. Dad, not to be outdone, decided he could come up with his own signature cheesy/creamy potato dish. We didn't see this one as often as Mom's, but when we did, it was just as welcome.*

Mix all ingredients except the cornflakes together in a large mixing bowl, then pour into a nonstick or greased 9 x 13-inch baking pan or casserole dish. Sprinkle the crushed cornflakes across the top.

Bake in a preheated 350°F oven for 45 to 60 minutes. Let stand for at least 5 minutes before serving.

1 pound baking potatoes, peeled, diced to ¼ inch, or 1 pound frozen hash browns, thawed

¼ cup unsalted butter or margarine, melted

¼ cup shredded onions

½ pint sour cream

½ 11-ounce can cream of chicken soup

¾ cup grated Cheddar cheese

½ teaspoon salt

⅛ teaspoon freshly ground pepper

1 cup crushed cornflakes or breadcrumbs

# Minted Fruit and Rice Salad

MAKES 4 SERVINGS

*SALADS HAVE ALWAYS BEEN a part of my family's life. It was a rare night that Mom set a table without a salad. But not just any old salad. She created salads with a special difference. I've shared her Mandarin Orange Salad in my first book. Here's a worthy addition to that, a salad that often found its way onto the holiday tables. It's a clean, tangy salad that complements chicken or turkey perfectly.*

⅔ cup pineapple juice

½ teaspoon salt

⅓ cup water

1 cup Minute Rice

1 10- to 11-ounce can mandarin orange slices, drained, or 3 clementines, sectioned

8 ounces crushed pineapple

½ cup chopped cucumber

½ cup chopped red onion

4 tablespoons chopped fresh mint

In a large, nonreactive saucepan, place the pineapple juice, salt and water and bring to a boil. Add the Minute Rice, remove from heat, cover and let stand according to the package directions.

Place the cooled rice in a large mixing bowl and add the mandarin orange slices, the pineapple, the cucumber and the red onion. Top with the mint and toss all.

# Asian Shrimp and Spinach Salad

MAKES 4 MAIN COURSE SERVINGS

*I'M A BIG FAN of spinach salads. If you have my first cookbook,* In the Kitchen with Bob, *you've probably tried my Korean Salad. But I'm also a fan of seafood (and my daughter Taylor absolutely adores shrimp), so it was natural that I'd start to play around with a spinach salad again, but with a seafood touch. What sets this one apart was adding the distinctively Asian sweet/sour twist. See what you think.*

## SALAD

- ½ pound fresh spinach, washed, stems removed
- 1 8-ounce can sliced water chestnuts, drained
- 1 large handful bean sprouts, washed, drained
- 2 hard-boiled eggs, chopped
- ½ pound medium shrimp, peeled, deveined, cooked, cut in half lengthwise

## DRESSING

- ½ cup soy sauce
- ½ cup vegetable oil
- 1 teaspoon hot chile sesame oil
- ½ teaspoon brown sugar

**FOR SALAD:** Place the spinach, water chestnuts, bean sprouts and hard-boiled eggs in a large wooden serving bowl and toss lightly. Place the shrimp around the bowl on top of the other ingredients.

**FOR DRESSING:** Mix the dressing ingredients in a blender, then pour over the salad and serve.

# Ten-Layer Salad

MAKES 8 SERVINGS

*MY BEST FRIEND and his wife gave Toni and me a cookbook for a wedding present. But it wasn't authored by some big-time chef or famous TV personality. It was a compendium of their best recipes, dishes that we'd been eating with them for years and raving about every time we had them. By far my favorite among favorites was Kathy's Ten-Layer Salad. It seems so simple, but wait until you put it on the table.*

2 cups chopped fresh spinach
4 hard-boiled eggs, chopped
3 slices bacon, crumbled
  Dash salt
  Dash freshly ground pepper
  Dash sugar
2 cups chopped romaine lettuce
1 cup frozen peas, thawed
1 cup chopped green onions (white and green parts)
1 cup mayonnaise
1 cup Miracle Whip
½ cup shredded Cheddar cheese
½ cup shredded carrots

In a 3- to 4-quart glass serving bowl, layer the first 9 ingredients, repeating the seasonings after adding the bacon. Mix the mayonnaise and Miracle Whip and spread on top like icing. Sprinkle with the Cheddar and carrots.

# Crepe Chalet Caesar Salad

MAKES 6 SERVINGS

*THIS IS THE CAESAR SALAD I made tableside at my restaurant, The Crepe Chalet, in Wilmington, Delaware. While the performance was surely one of the reasons people ordered the salad (I would make an almost vaudevillian escapade out of the preparation), I have since realized that it was the salad they were really interested in...as entertaining as I may have been. The appeal of this salad was, and still is, the intensity of its flavors.*

1 large and 1 small head romaine lettuce
1 garlic bulb, cloves peeled
½ cup vegetable oil
1 teaspoon dry mustard
1 tablespoon Worcestershire sauce
Salt and freshly ground pepper to taste
⅛ cup red wine vinegar
1 to 2 coddled eggs
½ teaspoon garlic salt
Juice of ½ lemon
Lightly seasoned croutons
Freshly grated Parmesan cheese
1 anchovy fillet (optional)

Wash the romaine in cold water, vigorously shake dry and spread on paper towels—the leaves must be dry, but not limp.

In a large, wooden (preferably teak) bowl, crush the garlic. Use a garlic press to do this, then scoop up the squashings and put them through the press again—the idea is to release as much garlic "liquid" as possible.

Add oil to about a 6-inch diameter on the bottom of the bowl (don't over-oil—you can always add more later). Sprinkle the dry mustard over the oil—a light dusting to color. Add the Worcestershire sauce, then with a fork combine all elements in the bowl to this point.

Add salt and pepper to taste and stir again, then add the vinegar and stir again. Then crack in 1 egg and whip the mixture. It should begin to gel and get loosely pudding-like. If not, add in another egg and whip again (never add more than 2 eggs). Shake in a tad of the garlic salt, then squeeze in the lemon juice. Whip again—the dressing will loosen up a bit with the juice, but that's O.K. as long as it isn't watery.

Break crisp, dry romaine into the bowl. Put in about half of it, toss, then add the rest and toss again. Add croutons and a little Parmesan. Toss again. Serve on dinner plates and sprinkle liberally with Parmesan. An anchovy fillet can be added on top of salad, if desired.

# Granny's Cole Slaw

MAKES 6 CUPS

*THERE ARE ONLY TWO THINGS that my wife Toni can't do without in the culinary world, and they're both creations of her grandmother. The first is Granny's Pot Roast (see recipe on page 38). The second is Granny's Cole Slaw. She makes it the same way Granny's made it for almost 70 years (and her mother 50 years before that), and I'll put it up against any slaw in the world. Be advised that this is one of the most valuable recipes we as a family own. Treasure it.*

1 1-pound head cabbage, chopped well

2 large carrots, finely chopped

1 small onion, finely chopped
Mayonnaise (Granny uses Kraft Real Mayonnaise) to desired consistency

1 tablespoon sugar
Salt to taste

Granny always chops her carrots and onions in a food processor, and shreds the cabbage in one as well. She likes a fine chop for those ingredients. You can either use a food processor or chop them all by hand.

Place the cabbage, carrots and onion in a large mixing bowl and add the mayonnaise to desired consistency. Then add the sugar and salt to taste. Chill before serving.

# Hot Crabmeat and Avocado Salad

*A MARRIAGE MELDS MANY THINGS. Besides the bride and groom, of course, there are the two families, who over time blend personalities, and histories, and hopes, and dreams...and cuisines and recipes. When the Bowersoxes and Parisis came together on September 11, 1988, crabmeat salad from my side met avocado salad from Toni's side, and voila. A new salad is born. Seriously, though, it was probably just a matter of not having enough bowls at a family gathering and the two salads "married." However it came about, it's a great union, and one I hope you'll love.*

| | |
|---|---|
| 1 | 7- to 8-ounce can crabmeat, drained, picked over |
| ⅓ | cup chopped celery |
| 3 | hard-boiled eggs, chopped |
| 2 | tablespoons chopped pimiento |
| 1 | tablespoon chopped onion |
| ½ | teaspoon salt |
| ½ | cup mayonnaise |
| 3 | large or 4 small ripe avocados |
| | Lemon juice |
| | Salt to taste |
| 3 | tablespoons dry breadcrumbs |
| 1 | teaspoon unsalted butter, melted |
| 2 | tablespoons slivered almonds |

Preheat the oven to 400°F. In a large mixing bowl, mix together the crab, celery, eggs, pimiento, onion, salt and mayonnaise. Set aside.

Cut the unpeeled avocado lengthwise in half and remove the pits. Brush each half with the lemon juice and sprinkle with a little salt. Fill the avocado halves with the crab mix. Toss the breadcrumbs in the butter and spoon over the crabmeat.

Place in an ungreased, shallow baking dish and bake uncovered for 10 minutes. Sprinkle the almonds over the crumb topping and bake 5 minutes longer or until bubbly.

# Tahini Salad Dressing

MAKES 8 OUNCES

*You know how restaurant "made-from-scratch" salad dressings are so incredible? Bright, tangy, complex concoctions that leave you wishing you could have the recipe? Well, this tahini is like that. It came from a dear friend back in my hippie days, when we put it on everything from lettuce to brown rice. It's easy to make and you'll be asked again and again to share the recipe with your dinner guests.*

½ cup tahini (sesame seed paste)

⅓ cup water

¼ cup vegetable oil

2 tablespoons lemon juice

½ teaspoon salt

1 tablespoon chopped green onions (white and green parts)

2 garlic cloves, crushed, minced

4 to 6 drops hot pepper sauce (such as Tabasco)

Place all ingredients in a blender and process on high until smooth.

NOTE: Also makes a great dip or sauce for vegetables.

# Sourdough Cheese Bread

MAKES 2 LOAVES

*Dad loved sourdough. He was a master at using it. He made the lightest, fluffiest pancakes on the planet with it. And he made the most spectacular breads. To me, his masterpiece was this Sourdough Cheese Bread. Toasted and buttered, with a little seasoned salt sprinkled on it...boy, that was it for me. I include his sourdough starter recipe here for you, if you need to get started.*

**FOR SOURDOUGH STARTER:** Dissolve the yeast in a small amount of lukewarm water. Stir the flour into the remaining water and add the yeast mix. Mix well and cover with a moist tea towel, and let it stand in a draft-free area that is 85°F or better (we've used the top of the refrigerator or the laundry dryer) for at least 6 hours.

**FOR PRIMARY BATTER:** Mix all ingredients together well. Return whatever you don't use (there should be about 1 quart) to the starter container for future use.

**FOR BREAD:** Let all ingredients come to room temperature before starting. Put the primary batter in a warm mixing bowl. Heat the milk to lukewarm, then stir it into the batter. Stir in the sugar and the salt. Beat the egg, then stir it into the batter, then add the melted butter. Stir well.

### QUICK OVERNIGHT SOURDOUGH STARTER

- 1  2¼ teaspoon-package plus 1 tablespoon dry yeast
- 4  cups lukewarm water
- 4  cups all-purpose flour

### PRIMARY BATTER

- 1  cup sourdough starter
- 2½  cups white flour
- 2  cups warm water

### BREAD

- 1½  cups primary batter
- 1  cup milk
- ¼  cup sugar
- 2  teaspoons salt
- 1  egg
- 2  tablespoons unsalted butter, melted
- 1½ to 1¾ cups grated sharp cheese
- 4  cups white flour (unbleached)
- 1  tablespoon unsalted butter, melted

Add the grated cheese and stir. Add the flour ½ cup at a time, stirring after each addition. When the dough has begun to pull away from the sides of the bowl, turn it out onto a floured surface and knead it until it is smooth and satiny. Shape it into loaves and place in greased loaf pans. Brush the tops with melted butter and cover the pans, setting them in a warm 85°F spot. Let them proof for about 2 hours or until doubled in size.

Bake in a preheated 375°F oven for 30 minutes. Be careful—this bread browns extremely easily. If it is getting too brown and the baking time is not over, cover the bread with a tent of aluminum foil to retard the browning action. When done, remove from the baking pans and place on wire racks to cool.

NOTE: There are special yeasts that you can purchase for sourdough starter. Dad got his from Sourdough Jack's Kitchen in San Francisco.

# Tuscan Bread

MAKES 1 LARGE ROUND LOAF, OR 2 REGULAR LOAVES

*My dad loved to bake, especially breads. He became fascinated with traditional breads early on, and spent a lot of time learning how to make them correctly. His fascination with Italian cuisine eventually led him to the classic Tuscan peasant breads (top, page 96). Bake yourself a loaf, put on some Pavarotti, pour some chianti, put out some olive oil to dip the bread in, and step back a few centuries....*

**SPONGE**

- 1 tablespoon dry yeast
- ½ cup lukewarm water
- ¾ cup flour

**DOUGH**

- 3½ cups flour
- ⅓ cup whole wheat flour
- 1 teaspoon salt (optional)
  Sponge
- 1⅓ cups lukewarm water

**FOR SPONGE:** Stir the yeast into the water in a bowl until it is dissolved. Let it stand until it looks foamy. Then add the flour and stir until combined well. Cover the bowl loosely with waxed paper or a tea towel and let the dough rise in a warm place until it has doubled (Dad always used his unheated oven with the door closed).

**FOR DOUGH:** Stir the flours and the salt (if using) together in a large bowl. Make a welled area in the center and pour in the sponge, then the water. Mix together well, beating vigorously about 4 minutes.

Place the dough onto a well-floured surface and knead vigorously for 10 minutes until it is smooth and elastic (it'll bounce back when you touch it). Form dough into a ball, lightly dust it with flour and place in a nonstick (or greased) bowl, cover with a tea towel and let it rise again in a warm place until doubled (this will take about an hour). Put dough on the floured surface again and flatten it into an oval, then roll it into an oblong loaf.

To bake it traditionally, place the loaf on a baking stone and bake in a preheated 450°F oven for 30 to 35 minutes. If you don't have a stone, use a cookie sheet and bake at 400°F for 45 to 50 minutes. In both cases, the bread is done when it gives off a "hollow" sound when tapped lightly on the side. Let cool on rack before handling.

# Granny's Polish Easter Bread

MAKES 2 LOAVES

*TONI'S GRANDMOTHER, MARTHA MARSHALL, has probably been making this bread (bottom, page 96) for almost 70 years. It's a recipe she inherited from her grandmother, and who knows how far back it goes in the old country before that. We call it "Granny Bread" around our house, and love it dearly (almost as much as we love Granny herself). We usually get her to make us a few loaves around each holiday, from Christmas through Easter. It's always a treat when she shows up with it. Getting the recipe for this book was hard, though. You see, Granny pretty much measures everything by hand or sight, so translating to measures was difficult. But I think we got it here, and offer it up to you and your descendents. Someday your great-, great-, great- grandchildren will be wondering how far back in your family history the recipe goes.*

| | |
|---|---|
| 1¼ | cups milk |
| ¾ | cup sugar |
| 6 | tablespoons unsalted butter |
| 3 | egg yolks |
| 1 | whole egg |
| 1 | teaspoon vanilla extract |
| 4 | cups bread flour |
| ¾ | teaspoon salt |
| 1½ | tablespoons orange zest |
| | Juice of ½ orange |
| 1½ | teaspoons yeast |
| 1 | cup golden raisins |

In a large saucepan over medium to medium-high heat, heat the milk (do not boil it). Remove from the heat and add the sugar and butter, stirring until they melt into the milk. Cool enough so that when you add the egg yolks and egg, they don't solidify. Mix the yolks, egg and vanilla extract into the liquid and stir to blend well.

Sift together the flour and salt, then gradually fold them into the liquid, beating enough to form a smooth batter. Fold in the orange zest and the orange juice and beat again just enough to blend. Add the yeast last, beating or kneading it into the dough. Place the dough into a large bowl, cover with a tea towel to keep it warm and let it rise long enough to double in size (an hour or more, usually).

Place the dough on a lightly floured surface and knead it down. Add the raisins and fold them into the dough, distributing them throughout. Place the dough in the bowl, cover again and let rise again for about an hour.

Divide the dough into 2 pieces and place in bread loaf pans. Bake in a preheated 350°F oven for an hour. Be sure to rotate the pans about a half hour into the baking (only if you have 1 pan on the top rack and 1 pan on the bottom rack).

NOTE: We love this bread as a breakfast bread, but it is also terrific as a sandwich bread, especially with sliced, baked Easter or Christmas ham and Polish beet-horseradish sauce.

# Jeanne's Scones

MAKES 12 3-INCH ROUNDS

*My Aunt Jeanne's scones are the real thing. Though we Bowersoxes are mostly German, there is about 2% of us that's Scot. That part comes from the McClellan side of the family (going back tangentially to General George McClellan of the Civil War). Jeanne has managed to hold onto that part of our heritage, including some of the great recipes like these scones.*

| | |
|---|---|
| 2 | cups flour |
| ¼ | teaspoon baking soda |
| 2½ | teaspoons baking powder |
| 1 | teaspoon salt |
| ¼ | cup sugar |
| ⅔ | cup milk |
| ⅓ | cup shortening |

Sift the dry ingredients together in a mixing bowl. Slowly add the milk and mix into a dough. Cut in the shortening.

Knead the dough. Pat down to about ½-inch thick and cut into 12 equal rounds. Place on a nonstick or lightly floured cookie sheet and bake in a preheated 400°F oven for about 15 minutes.

# DESSERTS
# & SWEETS

# The World's Best Cobbler

*THE CLAIM OF "WORLD'S BEST" is made by both my father and my brother, but both will tell you when pressed on the matter that the recipe is pure West Virginia—its heritage going back through my mother, to my grandmother and her housekeeper/cook Alice Anthony. I'm sure both Dad and Paul added their touches here and there, but the soul of the dish is still Mom's and her family's, and with every bite, this cobbler lives up to its name.*

1½  cups flour

2  teaspoons baking powder

2  tablespoons sugar

¼  teaspoon salt

½  cup (1 stick) unsalted butter

1  egg

½  cup milk

2  to 3 cups fruit (such as apples, blueberries, peaches or pears), peeled, cut into ⅛-inch-thick wedges

3  tablespoons sugar

3  tablespoons flour

2  tablespoons unsalted butter

Make the dough first, so it can rest while you do the other parts of the recipe. Sift together the flour, baking powder, sugar and salt. Add the ½ cup of butter and mix to the crumb stage. In a separate bowl, beat the egg with the milk and add it to the flour mixture and mix until a dough forms. Set aside.

Prepare the fruit. In a large bowl, mix the fruit with the 3 tablespoons of sugar and the 3 tablespoons of flour. Pour the fruit into an 8 x 8-inch baking dish, and dot here and there with the 2 tablespoons of butter, broken up.

Cover the fruit in the baking dish with the dough, and bake in a preheated 375°F oven for about 25 minutes. Serve hot with ice cream.

# Grumble's Pennsylvania Dutch Bread Pudding

MAKES 4 SERVINGS

*MY DAD'S REPUTATION as a great baker was never questioned by anyone who tasted his creations, but few were privy to the spectacle of the creation. He would disappear into the kitchen, dressed in his baggy pants, a flannel shirt, an apron wrapped around his ample middle, and his glasses perched precariously on the tip of his nose. And he would grumble. That's the only word for it. You could hear him mumbling to himself as he cooked, or grumbling along with the classical music station that he played whenever in the kitchen. Somewhere along the line, one of the grandkids began referring to him as "Grumbles," and the name stuck, so dear to us all over the years, that nothing else seems quite right anymore. This is one of his best creations, a dish that harkens back to his birth in York, Pennsylvania, the heart of the Amish and Pennsylvania Dutch world.*

3 eggs, beaten

2 tablespoons sugar

1 teaspoon salt

3 cups milk

4 cups cubed bread

2 tablespoons unsalted butter, melted

½ teaspoon ground cinnamon

¼ teaspoon ground nutmeg or freshly grated

¼ cup raisins

In a large mixing bowl, blend together the eggs, sugar, salt and milk. In a second bowl, place the bread, butter, cinnamon and nutmeg. Then gently stir the milk mixture into the bread mixture. Add the raisins and gently fold with your hands until thoroughly mixed.

Pour into a 1½-quart buttered casserole. Bake for 25 minutes in a preheated 350°F oven. Serve hot.

# Tiramisu of the Deities

MAKES 8 SERVINGS

*In Italian, tirami su literally means "pick me up." It is a rich dessert made from coffee-soaked biscuits layered with sweet mascarpone cheese. My brother Paul says he had this recipe bestowed upon him by "two venerable Italian ladies who knew what they were doing." It's not for the calorie-counter, obviously, but if you love tiramisu, then this is the real thing...a recipe blessed by heritage, authenticity, and if Paul's right, some higher powers as well.*

5 large egg yolks

⅓ cup sugar

½ cup sweet Marsala wine

1 tablespoon water

½ cup heavy cream

2 teaspoons vanilla extract

1 pound *mascarpone* cheese, room temperature

1 cup cooled espresso or strong coffee

3 tablespoons rum or brandy

3 tablespoons sugar

24 ladyfingers

5 ounces semi-sweet chocolate, grated

1 tablespoon cocoa powder

In a medium, heatproof bowl, using a whisk beat the eggs and the ⅓ cup sugar until pale yellow. Whisk in the Marsala wine and the water. Set the bowl in a deep skillet of barely simmering water and whisk the mixture until it reaches 160°F (use a baking thermometer to gauge this). Remove the bowl and cool 15 minutes, stirring frequently.

In another bowl, beat the cream with the vanilla extract until it forms soft peaks. Place the cheese in a third large bowl, and gently fold in the whipped cream and the cooled egg mixture.

In a small bowl, combine the espresso, rum and the remaining 3 tablespoons of sugar. Dip the ladyfingers into this mixture and arrange them in a 9 x 13-inch baking dish or casserole dish.

Spread ½ of the cheese mixture over the ladyfingers, and sprinkle with ½ of the grated chocolate. Repeat these 2 layers again, 1 on top of the other. Sprinkle the soft cocoa over all when done. Cover and refrigerate for 24 hours before serving.

# Charlotte's "Beat-Like-Hell" Chocolate Cake

MAKES 1 2-LAYER CAKE OR 1 SHEET CAKE

*CHARLOTTE BOWERSOX WAS MY grandmother on my father's side. She was the wife of Hixon Tracey Bowersox, a Lutheran minister, after whom I'm partially named—my middle name is Tracey. Hixon loved chocolate cake, especially this cake, because of its moistness and the icing, which isn't overly sweet like some can be. Charlotte died the year I was born, so I never knew her, but her recipe has been kept alive in all branches of the family. Dad nicknamed it "Beat-Like-Hell," because that is what Charlotte did to the batter, which, as the story is told in the family, is the secret to its uniqueness among chocolate cakes. I'm not aware of any connection between the name and my grandfather's calling, but you never know....*

- 2 cups sugar
- 8 tablespoons unsalted butter
- 2 eggs
- ½ cup cocoa
- ¾ cup hot water
- ¾ cup buttermilk or sour milk
- 1 teaspoon baking powder
- 1 teaspoon baking soda
- ½ teaspoon salt
- 2 cups flour

In a large mixing bowl, cream the sugar and butter together well. Add the eggs 1 at a time and beat to incorporate. Add the cocoa, then the hot water and buttermilk and mix well.

In a separate bowl, sift together the baking powder, baking soda, salt and flour. Gradually blend the 2 bowls together, and then "beat like hell," which means to vigorously beat the batter with a wooden spoon for several minutes. Your arm may get tired, but this is a specific instruction from Charlotte...gotta do it by hand, not by mixer.

Pour the batter into 2 greased and floured pans (or 1 sheet cake pan) and bake in a preheated 350°F oven for about 30 minutes or until a toothpick comes out clean when inserted into the center of the cake. Remove and cool before stacking and icing (see recipe page 107).

# Boiled Chocolate Icing

*THIS IS THE STUFF THAT REALLY MAKES Charlotte's cake, we believe. It's not as sickeningly sweet as commercial frostings, but it packs a real chocolate punch. It's also great for icing cupcakes, too.*

| | |
|---|---|
| 1½ | ounces unsweetened chocolate |
| ½ | cup sugar |
| ½ | cup boiling water |
| 1½ | tablespoons cornstarch |
| ⅛ | teaspoon salt |
| 3 | tablespoons water |
| 1½ | tablespoons unsalted butter, softened |
| 1 | teaspoon vanilla extract |

In a double boiler or a saucepan set inside another saucepan or skillet of water, melt the chocolate. Add in the sugar and the boiling water, then bring that mixture to a boil. As soon as it reaches boiling, move on. You'll have to work swiftly from here on.

Dissolve the cornstarch and salt in the 3 tablespoons of water, then stir into the just-boiling chocolate. Boil until you achieve a "spreadable" consistency, stirring constantly. Remove immediately from the heat and add in the butter and vanilla and stir until melted and absorbed into the frosting. Spread the frosting onto the cake very quickly, as it will set up and become more solid as it cools.

Desserts

# Colorado Fruit Tart

MAKES 8 TO 10 SERVINGS

*"BEAUTIFUL AND ORGASMIC" is how my sister Maggie describes this tart. Beautiful because once finished, it's almost too pretty to cut and serve. Orgasmic because of what its taste will do for you. It's a recipe that was passed around her place of work in Colorado. I'm glad it made it East of the Mississippi.*

## CRUST

- ½ cup almonds
- ½ cup (1 stick) unsalted butter, softened
- 2 tablespoons sugar
- 1½ cups all-purpose flour
- ½ teaspoon almond extract

## FILLING

- 1 8-ounce package cream cheese, softened
- 2 tablespoons Amaretto liqueur
- ½ teaspoon almond extract
- 3 tablespoons sugar
- 1 teaspoon vanilla extract

## GLAZE

- ½ cup apricot preserves or orange marmalade
- 1 tablespoon unsalted butter
- 1 tablespoon freshly squeezed lemon juice
- 2 tablespoons Amaretto liqueur

## TOPPING

- 3 to 4 cups fresh fruit in season (such as strawberries, blueberries, seedless grapes cut in half or clementines)

**FOR CRUST:** Preheat the oven to 350°F. Butter a 10-inch tart pan with a removable bottom. In a food processor or electric mixer, combine the ingredients for the crust. Press into the bottom and up the sides of the pan and chill for 30 minutes. Bake the crust for 20 to 25 minutes or until the shell is golden brown. Let cool on a rack before filling.

**FOR FILLING:** Mix all the filling ingredients until smooth and spread them over the cooled tart crust. Chill until firm.

**FOR GLAZE:** While the tart is chilling, place all of the ingredients for the glaze in a small saucepan and stir over heat until combined. Remove from heat and cool.

**FOR TOPPING:** Arrange the fruit in a circular pattern on the tart. Brush the fruit with the glaze. Chill well before serving.

# Paul's Hazelnut Cheesecake

MAKES 8 SLICES

*I WOULD HAVE TO SAY that if anyone in the family inherited Dad's instinct, talent and intuition for baking, it was my brother Paul. During the early 1980s, he turned that gift into a business, when he dominated the upscale dessert market in the restaurants of Denver, Colorado. He supplied most of the top restaurants with their mouthwatering desserts, and though he didn't choose to pursue that opportunity as a career, the legacy of that time is a number of five-star concoctions for the lovers of things sweet, sensual and sinful. He was way ahead of his time in the use of hazelnut, which makes this cheesecake stand in a class by itself. Try a slice with a cup of hot hazelnut coffee some afternoon.*

**CRUST**

- 1 cup graham cracker crumbs
- ¼ cup ground hazelnuts
- 8 tablespoons unsalted butter
- 1 tablespoon water

**FILLING**

- 3 8-ounce packages cream cheese, softened
- 1 cup sugar
- 4 eggs
- 1 teaspoon Frangelico (hazelnut liqueur)
- 16 ounces sour cream
- 1 cup heavy cream

**TOPPING**

- ½ cup coarsely chopped hazelnuts
- 3 tablespoons Frangelico

**FOR CRUST:** Preheat the oven to 350°F. Grease the sides and bottom of a 10-inch springform pan. Combine the graham cracker crumbs, hazelnuts, butter and water. Press the mixture into the bottom of the pan. Set aside.

**FOR FILLING:** In the bowl of an electric mixer, combine the cream cheese, sugar, 1 egg and Frangelico. Beat until smooth and creamy. Add the remaining eggs and the sour cream. Blend well. Add the heavy cream and beat until incorporated. Pour the mixture into the prepared pan and bake for 45 minutes.

After 45 minutes, turn off oven and allow cheesecake to sit in the closed oven for an additional 20 minutes. Remove from oven and allow to cool. Cover and chill in refrigerator.

**FOR TOPPING:** Combine the chopped hazelnuts and the Frangelico and pour the mixture over the top of the cold cheesecake.

# Baked Date Pudding

MAKES AN 8 x 8-INCH PAN

*WHEN DAD RETIRED from the DuPont company, he went into the kitchen and basically didn't come out again. He spent the last ten years of his life becoming the finest traditional baker I know (see some of his breads elsewhere in this book). Besides breads, he loved playing around with desserts, especially puddings. This recipe started out as a bread pudding, but evolved into a strictly date pudding. If you like bread puddings, give this version a try.*

| | |
|---|---|
| 1 | cup sugar |
| ½ | cup flour |
| ¼ | teaspoon salt |
| 1 | cup chopped dates |
| 1 | teaspoon vanilla extract |
| 2 | tablespoons milk |
| 3 | egg yolks |
| ⅓ | cup chopped walnuts |
| 3 | egg whites |
| 1½ | teaspoons baking powder |

In a large mixing bowl, mix together the sugar, flour, salt, dates, vanilla extract, milk, egg yolks and nuts. In a second bowl, beat the egg whites, and gently add in the baking powder and beat again briefly. Fold the egg whites into the pudding and blend well.

Pour the pudding into a buttered 8 x 8-inch baking pan or casserole dish. Place the baking dish in a larger pan filled with enough water to surround the baking dish on all sides. Bake in a preheated 350°F oven for 40 minutes. Let stand 15 minutes before serving, or chill for use later.

# Chocolate Pound Cake

MAKES 2 9 X 14-INCH LOAVES

*EVERYBODY LOVES POUND CAKE. There's nothing quite so good, smothered in strawberries or chocolate syrup. But what you usually get is the white pound cake, right? Now, while that's O.K. as far as pound cakes go, we Bowersoxes couldn't leave well enough alone, now could we? So here's what we came up with.*

3 cups sugar

1½ cups unsalted butter or shortening (such as Crisco)

5 eggs, beaten

½ teaspoon baking powder

3 cups flour

¼ teaspoon salt

½ to ⅔ cup cocoa

1 cup milk

1 teaspoon vanilla extract

Chocolate syrup

Confectioner's sugar

Preheat oven to 300°F. Bring all ingredients to room temperature. In a large mixing bowl, cream together the sugar and butter. Add the eggs 1 at a time, beating after each. Scrape down sides of bowl.

In a second mixing bowl, sift together the baking powder, flour, salt and cocoa. Alternately add the flour mixture and the milk, a little at a time of each, to the sugar, butter and egg mixture, beating to incorporate as you add each. After all the flour and milk is blended in, add the vanilla extract and blend in well.

Pour into a greased and lightly floured loaf pan or Bundt pan and bake in a 300°F oven for 1½ to 2 hours or until a toothpick inserted into the center of the cake comes out clean. Serve on individual dessert plates, drizzled with chocolate syrup and dusted with confectioner's sugar.

# Mamaw's Blueberry Buckle

MAKES 12 4-INCH SQUARES

*WE CALLED OUR MATERNAL GRANDMOTHER Mamaw. I'm not sure where it came from—probably one of us grandkids couldn't say "Grandmother," and that was that. Mamaw was a remarkable woman, and according to Dad, the woman who taught him almost all he knew about baking (the other woman he credits with mentorship was Alice Anthony, Mamaw's cook and housekeeper in her later years—Mamaw lived to be 98, but Alice carried on with her recipes). Though I never got to see Mamaw bake herself, I remember Dad raving about many of her dishes, this buckle in particular. I still have Mamaw's original recipe card in her handwriting. And it still tastes as good as we all remember it.*

## BUCKLE

- ¾ cup sugar
- ¼ cup shortening (such as Crisco)
- 1 egg
- ½ cup milk
- 2 cups flour
- 2 teaspoons baking powder
- ½ teaspoon salt
- 2 cups blueberries, washed, picked through

## TOPPING

- ½ cup sugar
- 1 cup sifted flour
- ½ teaspoon ground cinnamon
- ¼ cup unsalted butter, softened

**FOR BUCKLE:** In a mixing bowl, thoroughly combine the sugar, shortening and egg. Add in the milk and blend.

In a second bowl, sift together the flour, baking powder and salt. Add the blueberries and stir into the sugar and milk mixture. Combine well. Pour the batter into a greased 9-inch-square pan.

**FOR TOPPING:** Mix the sugar, flour, cinnamon and butter together in a mixing bowl and sprinkle evenly over the buckle. Bake in a preheated 375°F oven for 45 to 50 minutes. Cool for about 5 minutes before serving.

# Alice Duhon's Pralines

MAKES 50 CANDIES

*My first cousin, Susie Wilson, married into the Duhon clan of Louisiana. Ron Duhon, her husband, is as Cajun as they come, and one of the nicest guys on the planet. When Sue married him, she also married a rich heritage of fabulous food. I could do an entire book of recipes just from Sue and Ron, but for the moment, I thought I'd add in Sue's mother-in-law Alice's classic praline recipe. Alice Duhon makes upwards of 50 pounds of candies every Christmas, and this recipe is generations old. You won't find better Cajun pralines anywhere commercially. As Sue says, they're a little tricky to pull off, but they are spectacular—guar-an-teed.*

2 cups sugar

4 tablespoons light corn syrup

1 cup condensed milk

1 cup water (use milk can, so you get all remnants)

1 tablespoon unsalted butter

½ tablespoon vanilla extract

4 to 6 cups pecans (whole and broken pieces)

In a large saucepan over medium-high to high heat, mix and melt the sugar, corn syrup, milk and water. Make sure you have a large pan, because the mixture will boil up and take up a lot more space than you think.

Drop the heat to medium, and begin to stir constantly until the candy is firm, but not rolling into a hard ball. Remove from the heat and immediately add the butter, vanilla extract and the pecans. Beat this by hand until the candy holds its shape when some is dropped onto waxed paper. Drop a teaspoon at a time onto the waxed paper, but work fast...it stiffens up very quickly. Let it cool before breaking up and eating.

NOTE: If you find that the candy is setting up before you can get it onto the waxed paper, just reheat in the saucepan with a little more milk added and try again.

# Toffee Chocolate Squares

MAKES 2 POUNDS

*TOFFEE HAILS FROM the early 19th century. The original word in the Scottish dialects was "taffy," but we Americans hijacked that for our seashore treat. Early English toffee lovers called it "stickjaw," for obvious reasons. It wasn't until the 1930s that we started seeing toffee candies created for the American sweet tooth. This recipe is better than any commercial bar you can buy. I found it buried in the kitchen box I inherited from my grandmother and mother. I could have guessed that Mom had her hand in this one. After all, it's loaded with chocolate, isn't it?*

Graham crackers (broken into pieces, not crumbs)

1¼ cups dark brown sugar

1 cup (2 sticks) unsalted butter

2 tablespoons water

1 teaspoon vanilla extract (optional)

1 11½-ounce package milk chocolate chips

1 cup ground pecans (optional)

Line a 9 x 13-inch baking pan with aluminum foil. Smooth it across the bottom of the pan and up the sides. Arrange the graham cracker pieces all over the bottom of the pan. They can overlap each other a little, but don't stack them. Set aside.

In a nonstick saucepan over medium-high to high heat, blend together the brown sugar, butter and water, and stirring constantly, bring to a boil. Stir often so the mixture doesn't burn. You want to get it to what is called the "soft-crack stage," where a drop of the syrup dropped into ice water will separate into threads that are hard, but not brittle. This is around 285°F to 290°F. Immediately remove from the heat and add the vanilla extract (if using). Stir quickly, then pour the toffee mixture evenly into the pan over the graham crackers.

Immediately scatter the chocolate chips over the toffee and press them lightly with the back of a spatula so they begin to melt. When they are sufficiently melted, spread them out over the toffee, almost like an icing. Sprinkle with the nuts (if using). Cool completely before breaking up into pieces.

# Marilee's "To-Die-For" Chocolate Fudge

MAKES ABOUT 2 POUNDS

*You always knew when Mom had made her fudge. You'd come in the door and the whole house smelled like it was made of chocolate. Though she would sample any commercial fudges that crossed her path, she would invariably end up making her own, because, as she put it once, "no one else makes a fudge I'd be willing to die for." Here's the recipe she perfected to achieve that goal.*

3 cups sugar

1 cup heavy cream

4 tablespoons unsweetened cocoa powder (such as Van Hourten's)

1 tablespoon light corn syrup

1 tablespoon unsalted butter, softened

1 teaspoon vanilla extract

Place the sugar, cream, cocoa and corn syrup in a saucepan and heat over low heat, stirring constantly until smooth. Keep fudge mixture on enough heat to get it to start to bubble (don't let it start to boil—it should *just* bubble).

Take a teaspoon tip's worth of the fudge mixture and drop it into a cup of water. If the fudge forms a soft ball instead of melting into the water, the fudge is ready for the next step.

Remove the fudge from the heat and gently stir in the butter. Stir well, to incorporate the butter throughout. Add in the vanilla extract while stirring.

Pour the fudge into a pre-buttered baking tin (Mom used a 9 x 9-inch pan—she liked her fudge thick). Set on a rack and let cool. When cooled and hardened, cut into squares.

# Frozen Mocha Tort

*OH, THE SIN OF IT ALL! I mean, look at this thing! Macaroons, chocolate ice cream, hot fudge sauce, coffee ice cream, toffee bars...is there any question at all that it was created by my mother? No one who knew her and her love of any of these devilishly tempting ingredients would bet against it. It's a frozen dessert like no other.*

1 cup crumbled crispy macaroon cookies

2 tablespoons unsalted butter, melted

3 cups chocolate ice cream, softened but not melted

½ cup hot fudge sauce, cooled

3 cups coffee ice cream, softened but not melted

4 ounces chocolate-coated toffee candy bars, crushed

Combine the cookie crumbs and the butter in a bowl, then press into the bottom of a 9- or 10-inch springform pan. Bake in a preheated 350°F oven for 8 minutes or until brown. Set aside to cool.

Spread the chocolate ice cream over the cooled crust. Drizzle half of the chocolate sauce over that, then place in the freezer until firm.

Remove from the freezer and top the frozen layers with a layer of the softened coffee ice cream. Sprinkle that with the crushed candy bars and drizzle the rest of the sauce over the top and sides of the crust. Replace in the freezer until firm.

# Ice Cream Pie

MAKES 8 SERVINGS

*THIS RECIPE COMES FROM my Aunt Jeanne Wilson's family. It's so easy to make, yet it tops any of those other commercial ice cream cakes and pies you can buy. Whenever there's a family dinner planned, someone on the Wilson side can be expected to bring this pie. Or, if we're lucky, two of them might show up.*

Butter

1 9-inch pie shell

18 Oreo cookies, crushed

⅓ cup unsalted butter, melted

1 tablespoon unsalted butter

2 squares unsweetened chocolate

½ cup sugar

½ cup evaporated milk

1 quart ice cream (vanilla, chocolate, strawberry or mint chocolate chip), softened but not melted and runny

Whipped cream for topping

Grated chocolate for garnish (optional)

Carefully butter the pie shell. In a large mixing bowl, mix the cookies and the ⅓ cup butter until combined. Press into the buttered pie shell. Set aside.

Melt the 1 tablespoon of butter together with the squares of chocolate, the sugar and the evaporated milk in a nonstick saucepan. Cook over medium-low heat until a syrup forms. Remove from heat and cool, but don't let it get hard or difficult to pour.

Spread the softened ice cream into the pie shell, making sure you don't disturb the crust and put in freezer. After the pie has been frozen for 1 hour, cover the ice cream with the chocolate syrup and immediately place in the freezer for an additional hour.

When ready to serve, remove from freezer, top with whipped cream and cut into serving sizes. You can sprinkle with grated chocolate, if desired.

# Southern Sweet Chocolate Pie

*DID I MENTION my mother loved chocolate? Anytime, anyplace, any form. Here's a recipe she grew up on in West Virginia, a creamy delight created by her mother's mother long ago. I found the recipe written in my mother's youthful handwriting on a tattered, disintegrating piece of old stationery that smelled like my grandmother's West Virginia kitchen. It's easy to understand how Mom developed her taste for chocolate, given her exposure to Dixie delicacies like this.*

| | |
|---|---|
| 1 | 4-ounce package sweet cooking chocolate |
| ¼ | cup unsalted butter |
| 1⅔ | cups evaporated milk |
| 1½ | cups sugar |
| 3 | tablespoons cornstarch |
| ⅛ | teaspoon salt |
| 2 | eggs |
| 1 | teaspoon vanilla extract |
| 1 | unbaked 10-inch pie shell |
| 1⅓ | cups flaked coconut |
| ½ | cup chopped pecans |
| | Whipped cream or other whipped topping for garnish |

In a nonstick saucepan over low heat, mix the chocolate and the butter, stirring constantly until well blended. Remove from the heat and gradually blend in the evaporated milk.

In a mixing bowl, mix together the sugar, cornstarch and salt. Add the eggs and vanilla and beat until blended. Pour in the chocolate mixture and stir until blended well. Pour this mixture into the pie shell. Combine the coconut and the pecans and sprinkle them over the filling.

Place the pie in a preheated 375°F oven and bake for 45 to 50 minutes or until the pie is puffed and browned. Cover the pie loosely with foil during the last 15 minutes if the topping browns too quickly. Cool for at least 4 hours before serving. Garnish with dollops of freshly prepared whipped cream.

# Margie's Peanut Butter Fudge

MAKES 2½ POUNDS

*My Aunt Margie Fredericks loved fudge just about as much as my mother did. But while she liked Mom's "To-Die-For" Chocolate Fudge, Margie's special temptation was peanut butter fudge. I'm told that it took marathon negotiations, but eventually, Mom and Margie traded recipes, and both sides of the family were able to enjoy each other's sinful, fudgy pleasures. For peanut butter lovers, it doesn't get better than this.*

4½ cups sugar

1 12-ounce can evaporated milk
or 12 ounces cream

8 tablespoons unsalted butter

1 cup peanut butter

8 ounces marshmallow creme

1 teaspoon vanilla extract

In a saucepan over low heat, mix together the sugar, milk and butter. Keep the fudge mixture on just enough heat to get it to start to bubble (don't let it start to boil—it should just bubble).

Take a teaspoon tip's worth of the fudge mixture and drop it into a cup of water. If the fudge forms a soft ball instead of melting into the water, the fudge is ready for the next step.

Remove from the heat and add the peanut butter, marshmallow creme and vanilla extract. Beat until the mixture starts to thicken, then pour into a buttered 9 x 13-inch baking pan. Let cool, then cut into squares.

Aunt Margie and her
constant companion, Shadow

Desserts

# Mamaw's Lemon Cake

MAKES 8 SLICES

*THERE MAY NOT BE a simpler member of the cake pantheon than the lemon cake. But none I've ever had has matched the taste of this one my grandmother—we called her "Mamaw"—made. I've given you her lemon icing recipe, but she often topped this cake with a rich, creamy, dark chocolate icing when the mood struck (or when a little choco-holic named Bobby begged her to).*

**CAKE**

- ¾ cup unsalted butter or other shortening
- 1½ cups sugar
- 3 eggs, beaten
- 3 cups sifted cake flour
- 4 teaspoons baking powder
- ¾ teaspoon salt
- ⅓ cup fresh lemon juice
- ⅔ cup milk
- Grated rind of 1 lemon

**ICING**

- ½ cup (1 stick) unsalted butter
- ½ cup shortening
- 1½ teaspoons lemon extract
- 5½ cups confectioner's sugar
- ¼ cup plus 1 tablespoon milk
- Threads of lemon zest for garnish (optional)

**FOR CAKE:** Cream the butter and sugar in a mixing bowl, then add in the beaten eggs. Mix well, then add the remaining ingredients. Beat until smooth.

Pour into 2 greased and lightly floured 8- or 9-inch-round cake pans and bake in a preheated 350°F oven for 25 to 30 minutes or until a toothpick inserted into the center of the cake comes out clean. Cool on racks before removing from pans and icing.

**FOR ICING:** Cream the butter and shortening together in a mixing bowl. Add the extract and gradually add the sugar and the milk a little at a time (add more or less milk for the desired consistency of the icing). Stack the 2 layers of cake on a cake or serving plate, and evenly spread the icing over all. Garnish with threads of lemon in the center of the cake, if desired.

# Index

My partner, Rick Patterson, and
me at The Crepe Chalet, 1978

Left: Two of my closest QVC family—Paul Kelley and Judy Crowell

Above: Kathy Levine and I have been close friends since the first day at QVC, November 24, 1986

The Bowersox recipe box

## Somethin' Good

From the kitchen of **Wendy B.** serves **8-10**

Hot Chicken Salad

- cooked rice (3)
- diced cooked chicken (whole)
- 3 hard boiled eggs
- all onion
- lemon juice
- salt
- celery
- water chestnuts (1 can)
- mayonaise
- mushroom soup

## German Hamburgers

Bread Dough (3 loafs frozen, each cut in 8 pieces)

- Hamburger
- 1 lrg. cabbage
- onion

> We also enjoy garlic, green pepper in ours.

Brown hamburger, add chopped cabbage and onion, cover on to Steam cabbage and cook until tender. Cool to warm and drain grease. Cut dough in squares and stretch as possible. Put meat mixture in, tuck under to form a (on the bottom) Place on greased cookie sheet.

Bake at 350° for 30 minutes

## GARLIC CHEESE BREAD

- to 2½ cups flour
- tablespoon sugar
- teaspoons salt
- to 2 teaspoons finely chopped garli-
- package active dry yeast
- cup milk
- cup (4 oz.) shredded cheddar chee

1 TSP OREGANO

Combine 1 cup flour, sugar, salt,
Heat milk and cheese until milk is
Add to flour mixture. Beat until
Gradually stir in remaining flour
Knead until smooth - about 5 minu
Place in greased bowl, turning to
until double in size - about
Punch down, shape into loaf, and
Cover and let rise until double
0 for 45 to 50 minu

## STEAM DRESSING

cheese and then think
ency easy to pour into

on chopped fine.
two of Wor. Sauce, Tobasco.
cheese, to dressing.

sprinkle with finely

## FANTASY FUDGE

- 3 c. SUGAR
- 3/4 c. MARGARINE
- 2/3 c. (5⅓ oz. CAN) EVAP. M
- 1 12 oz. PKG. SEMI-SWEET C
- 1 7 oz. JAR KRAFT MARSHMAL
- 1 c. CHOPPED NUTS

T = tablespoons

Here's what's cookin'  Apple Pudding
Recipe from the kitchen of  About 2 lbs.

- 1½ c flour
- 3 T butter
- 2 tsp sugar
- ½ c milk
- ¼ tsp
- 1½ tsp
- ½ tsp
- 2 t

Mix all dry ingredien
butter & mix, then
peeled apples in baking dish
Add lemon season apples to Tac
dough mixture on top. Bake

## Ice Bax Cookies

- 1 c. soft shortening
- 3/4 1/2 c. sugar
- 3/4 1/2 c. packed brown sugar
- 2 3/4 c. sifted flour
- 2 eggs
- ½ tsp. soda
- 1 tsp. salt
- 2½ tsp. cin